The Zen Poems
of Ryōkan

PRINCETON LIBRARY OF ASIAN TRANSLATIONS

Advisory Committee for Japan:
Marius Jansen, Earl Miner, James Morley, Thomas J. Rimer

For Other Books in the Series See Page 220

The Zen Poems of Ryōkan

SELECTED AND TRANSLATED WITH
AN INTRODUCTION, BIOGRAPHICAL SKETCH,
AND NOTES
By Nobuyuki Yuasa

PRINCETON UNIVERSITY PRESS
PRINCETON, NEW JERSEY

COPYRIGHT © 1981 BY PRINCETON UNIVERSITY PRESS

PUBLISHED BY PRINCETON UNIVERSITY PRESS, PRINCETON, NEW JERSEY
IN THE UNITED KINGDOM: PRINCETON UNIVERSITY PRESS, GUILDFORD, SURREY

ALL RIGHTS RESERVED

LIBRARY OF CONGRESS CATALOGING IN PUBLICATION DATA WILL BE
FOUND ON THE LAST PRINTED PAGE OF THIS BOOK

PUBLICATION OF THIS BOOK HAS BEEN AIDED BY THE PAUL MELLON FUND OF
PRINCETON UNIVERSITY PRESS

THIS BOOK HAS BEEN COMPOSED IN LINOTRON BEMBO

CLOTHBOUND EDITIONS OF PRINCETON UNIVERSITY PRESS BOOKS
ARE PRINTED ON ACID-FREE PAPER, AND BINDING MATERIALS ARE
CHOSEN FOR STRENGTH AND DURABILITY

PRINTED IN THE UNITED STATES OF AMERICA BY PRINCETON
UNIVERSITY PRESS, PRINCETON, NEW JERSEY

To S., F., and A.

CONTENTS

ACKNOWLEDGMENTS	ix
LIST OF ILLUSTRATIONS	xi
INTRODUCTION	3
MAP OF THE RYŌKAN COUNTRY	4
BIOGRAPHICAL SKETCH	23
CHINESE POEMS	43
JAPANESE POEMS	107
DEWDROPS ON A LOTUS LEAF	169
EXPLANATORY NOTES	183
GLOSSARY OF PROPER NAMES	189
SELECTED BIBLIOGRAPHY	217

ACKNOWLEDGMENTS

MY HEARTFELT THANKS are due to Professors Earl Miner, William H. McCullough, and Helen Craig McCullough, without whose assistance the book would have never taken its present form, and to Professor Elizabeth Schultz who kindly read my manuscript and gave me valuable suggestions. The bulk of the translation was done by 1974, and in the process of bringing the book to its final shape I have relied rather heavily on the support of my friends. Although I hesitate to mention their names here, I should like to thank them with all my heart. My thanks are due also to the Ryōkan Museum at Izumozaki and to Niigata Prefectural Library for permitting me to use the portraits of Ryōkan reproduced here, and to Mr. Motochika Kimura for allowing me to reproduce samples of Ryōkan's calligraphy from his collection. I am also indebted for the photography to Mr. Masayoshi Nakamata. Last but not least, to Miss R. Miriam Brokaw of Princeton University Press I owe my gratitude for her warm interest in my work and her untiring cooperation.

NOBUYUKI YUASA
Hiroshima 1980

LIST OF ILLUSTRATIONS

1. Chinese poem in Ryōkan's handwriting	2
2. Portrait of Ryōkan by Miyagawa Rokusai, painted in 1830	24
3. Certificate granted by the priest Kokusen to Ryōkan	30
4. Chinese poem by Ryōkan (No. 6 in the text)	44
5. Chinese poem by Ryōkan (No. 14 in the text)	48
6. Chinese poem by Ryōkan (No. 123 in the text)	79
7. Japanese poem by Ryōkan (No. 217 in the text)	108
8. Japanese poem by Ryōkan (No. 233, 2nd envoy in the text)	113
9. Confucian maxim in Ryōkan's handwriting	182
10. Gogōan, the cottage where Ryōkan lived from 1804 to 1816	219

MAPS
1. The Ryōkan country 4
2. Japan 5

The Zen Poems
of Ryōkan

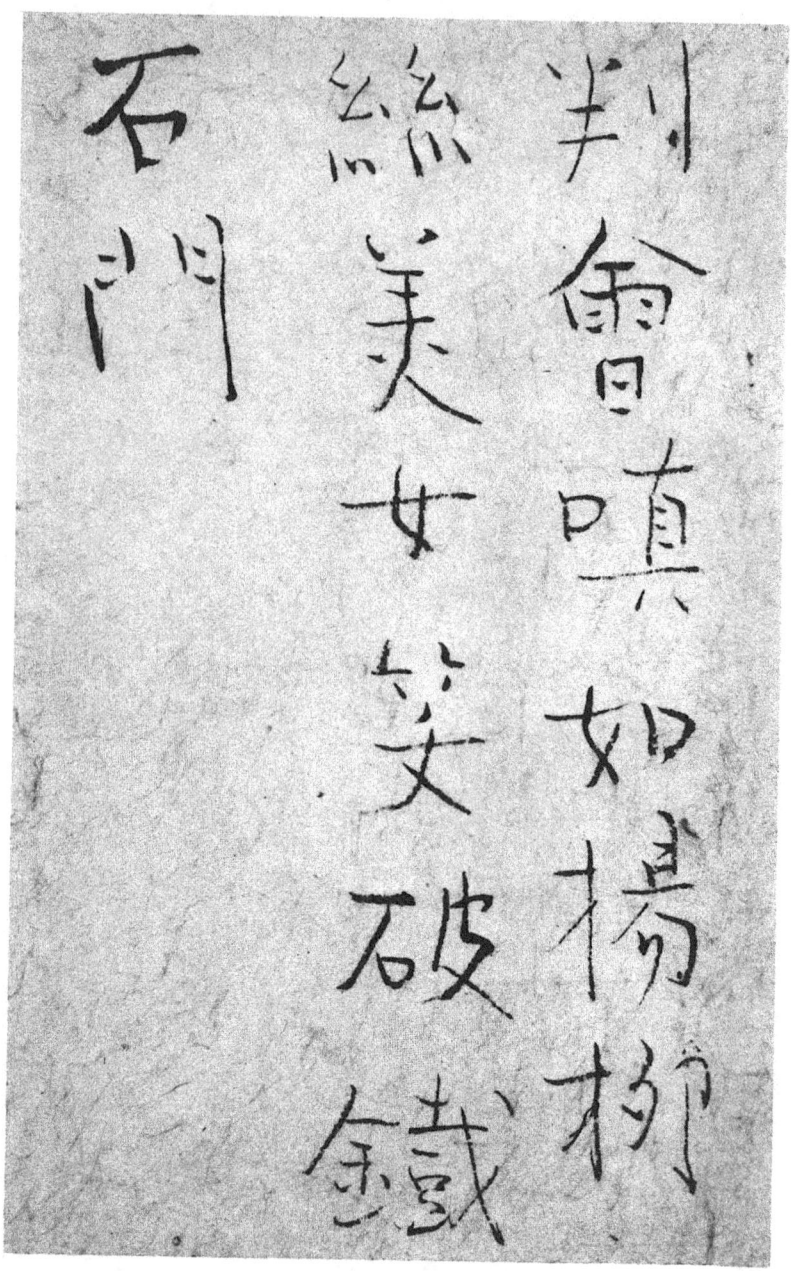

1. Chinese poem in Ryōkan's handwriting:
Han Kai's anger was softer than the thread of a willow branch,
A woman's smile is strong enough to blast stone or iron gates.

INTRODUCTION

RYŌKAN (1758-1831) is a poet-priest of the late Edo period. Among his more famous contemporaries are the *haikai* poet Kobayashi Issa (1763-1827), the romance writer Takizawa Bakin (1767-1848), and the historian Rai San'yō (1780-1832). Ryōkan lived as a recluse for most of his life, and left some fourteen hundred *waka* (Japanese poems), four hundred *kanshi* (Chinese poems), and a small number of *hokku*. As a person, he is often regarded as an eccentric who lived outside the pale of this world. This view owes its origin to the testimony of his contemporaries and of early writers who wished to exaggerate his unusualness, and in spite of the efforts of Sōma Gyofū (1883-1950) and other scholars who have tried to humanize his image, Ryōkan still remains an eccentric in the popular mind. The biographical sketch that follows this introduction is an attempt to correct that view, and to argue that Ryōkan's greatness depends not so much on his unusualness as on his deep understanding of himself and of the world around him.

Ryōkan's position in the literary history of Japan is often regarded as being open to dispute. The Edo period is generally said to be characterized by the rise of the merchant class, which led to the popularity of *haikai*, *kabuki*, and prose romances. Ryōkan shows little interest in any of these new genres so characteristic of his age. In my opinion, however, we must be cautious not to treat him as a literary anomaly. In the first place, Ryōkan is not alone in having attempted to rise above the level of popular culture. A classic example is Matsuo Bashō (1644-1694), who succeeded in refining *haikai* by attempting to correct vulgar words (*zokugo o tadasu*). In the second place, Ryōkan's indebtedness to popular culture is greater than it seems. He certainly worked within the limits of traditional forms, but by the frequent use of colloquialism and humble images, he infused them with freshness and vigour equal to those found in the most popular writers of his age. This double response to popular culture is what Ryōkan shares with many of the important writers of his time. Finally, his adherence to traditional forms places him in the long line of classical poets, both Japanese and Chinese. Therefore, it is only by evaluating his literary achievements against their background that we can fully appreciate his poetic greatness.

The *waka* of the Edo period is characterized by a tendency to break away from the rigid rules of composition handed down over many generations by professional teachers. This hardening of the courtly tradition

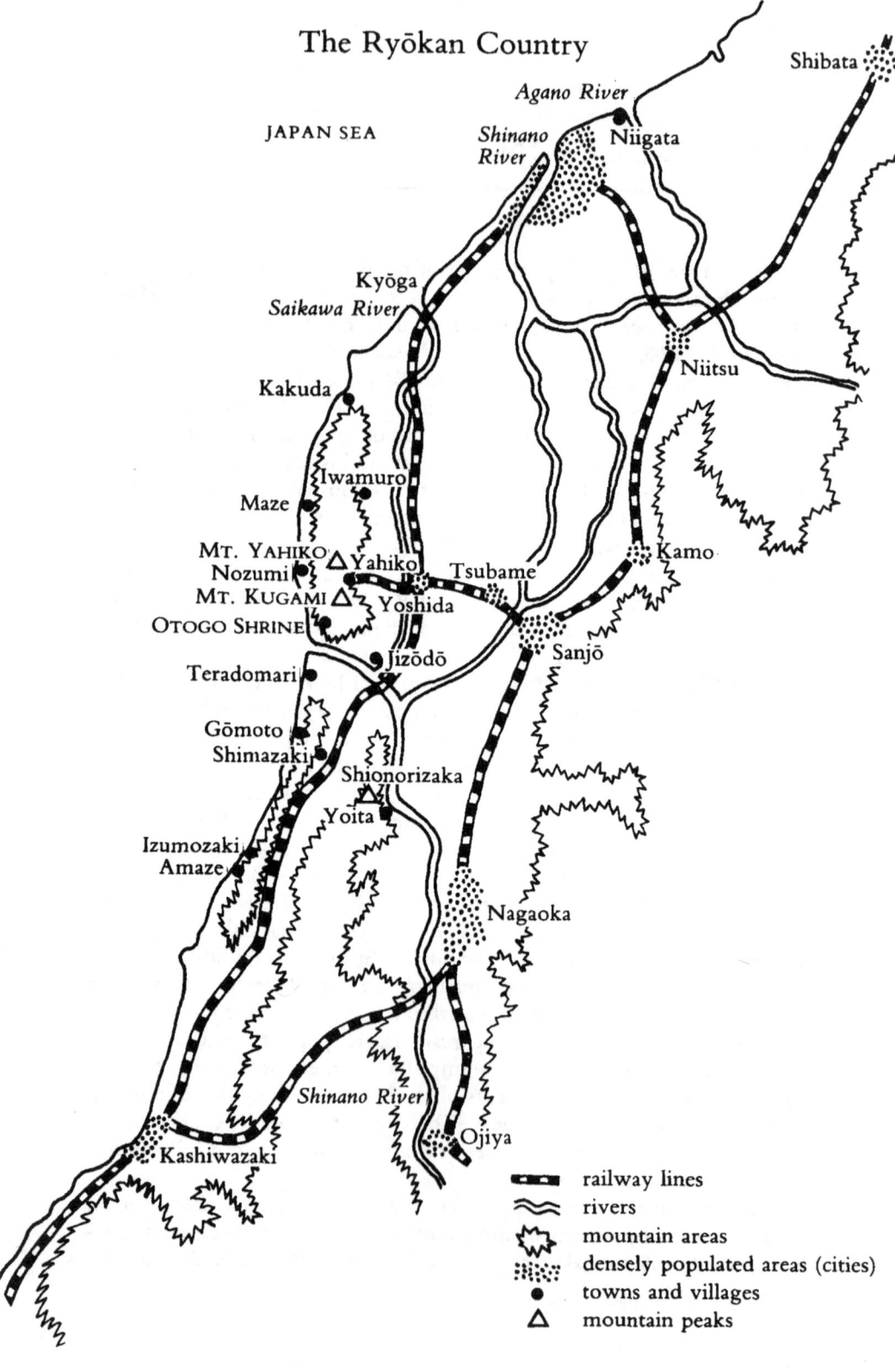

took place in the late Heian period. Fujiwara no Teika (1162-1241) resisted this trend. He says in *Eiga Taigai* that he needed no professional teachers in his study of *waka*, and that the works of ancient poets alone were a sufficient guide for him; but Kamo no Chōmei (1155-1216) reports in *Mumyōshō* of the priest Tōren that, after learning the name of an unusual plant from a teacher, he took special pride in his knowledge. In 1275, when the Fujiwara family split into three houses at the death of Fujiwara no Tameie (1198-1275), rivalry between the houses accelerated the process of hardening so much that the initiation by a teacher into the mysteries of poetic art, known as *Kokin denju*, became a kind of credential for a poet. The poets and critics of the Edo period, however, went against this tendency and upheld sincerity of feeling and expression as a literary value. For example, Kamo no Mabuchi (1697-1769) says in *Kaiko* that whenever one has an emotion in one's heart, one voices it spontaneously, producing poetry. Kagawa Kageki (1768-1843) also expresses a similar view when he says in *Niimanabi Iken* that poetry is a stream of melodiousness arising from the emotion in the heart. Motoori Norinaga (1730-1801) is of the opinion that poetry is produced when the human heart is moved by the beauty of things. Mabuchi's critical term, *makoto* (sincerity), Kageki's critical term, *shirabe* (melodiousness), and Norinaga's critical term, *mono no aware* (intense feelings roused by the beauty of things) are different in their implications, but they indicate that these critics shared a common premise in their discussion of poetry.

These critics, however, differed widely in their opinions as to which of the traditional anthologies should be taken as a guide—a point of great importance in determining their aesthetic attitudes. Mabuchi recommended imitation of the masculine style (*masuraoburi*) of the *Man'yōshū*. Kageki was opposed to the conscious imitation of any of the old styles but thought that the *Kokinshū* was better than any other anthology as a model. Norinaga maintained that the art of poetry reached its height in the *Shinkokinshū*, and that the best poems of this anthology were doubly recommendable, for they had the flower and fruit together (*kajitsu sōgu*). If we see Ryōkan's position against the background of this critical situation, perhaps we can say that it was closest to that of Mabuchi, for a number of letters Ryōkan wrote to his friends express his genuine interest in the *Man'yōshū*. According to the testimony of Kera Yoshishige (1810-1859), Ryōkan is reported to have said that a student of poetry should study the *Man'yōshū*, but that there was no need to study any other anthology, the *Kokinshū* being merely acceptable, and the *Shinkokinshū* not even worth reading. Furthermore, we know that Ryōkan borrowed and read the commentary on the *Man'yōshū* written by Katō Chikage (1735-1808), so probably the influence of Mabuchi reached him through this book. We also know that Ryōkan was in touch with Ōmura Mitsue (1753-1816), a disciple of Mabuchi, who left an account of his visit with Ryōkan. Thus, Ryōkan's proximity to Mabuchi and his school, at least in his critical stance, must be accepted.

It would be a great mistake, however, to regard Ryōkan as a mere *Man'yō* revivalist. For him, the *Man'yōshū* was a source of poetic inspiration rather than a model for conscious imitation. Ryōkan had none of Mabuchi's scholarly punctiliousness. Kera Yoshishige reports that Ryōkan disliked the works of professional calligraphers and poets, with their writing on prescribed themes. It is true that Mabuchi himself was far from being a purist in his practice, but when he imitated the *Man'yō* style, he did so with the precision of an archaeologist. For example, his *chōka* on Mt. Fuji (No. 263 in *Kinsei Wakashū*, Nihon Koten Bungaku Taikei, Iwanami Shoten, 1966) reads almost like a replica of a poem on the same subject by Yamabe no Akahito (d. c.736). Let me quote here the first of the two envoys as evidence.

Suruga naru / Fuji no takane wa / ikazuchi no / oto suru kumo no / ue ni koso mire.

> Here in Suruga,
> The peak of Mount Fuji soars
> Exceeding the clouds
> Thunder-rolling without cease,
> Just as we should all see it.

This is a beautiful imitation, but I think it is undeniable that there is a certain stiffness, coming from Mabuchi's classicism, which in an ironic way alienates him from the spirit of the *Man'yōshū*. By contrast, Ryōkan's approach is wholly unsystematic and seems at first sight a hit-or-miss affair. Let us take his *chōka* on the begging bowl (219 in the text) as an example. A passage in the middle reads:

Karigomo no / omoi midare te / yūzutsu no / kayuki kakuyuki / taniguku no / sawataru sokohi / amagumo no / mukafusu kiwami / ametsuchi no / yoriai no kagiri. . .

> Like the sea-tangle,
> My heart is tossed by fancies.
> Like the early star,
> I must start, and search it out,
> Be it in the hole

> Where toads lie in murky haunts,
>   Or hidden beneath
> Those darksome clouds lingering
>   Near the horizon,
> Where land and sky come together. . .

In this passage, the first two lines were probably taken from the *Man'yōshū*, No. 697, by Ōtomo no Katami (fl. 772), the second two from No. 196 by Kakinomoto no Hitomaro (fl. 680-700), the following four from No. 800 by Yamanoue no Okura (c. 660-733), and the last two from No. 1074 by Tanabe no Sakimaro (fl. 748). Although other sources for these lines are possible, I think it is obvious that Ryōkan took different expressions from different poets and put them all together. In my opinion, the greatest inspiration for Ryōkan in these lines was Hitomaro, who excelled in the elevated expression of his own feelings; but Ryōkan does not imitate him in the way Mabuchi imitates Akahito. In one of his Chinese poems (55 in the text), Ryōkan says, "Gleaning some words from old masters, I make my own poems." In my opinion, this is exactly what Ryōkan does in this passage, and in most of his other poems. What makes him great, however, is that in spite of his extensive borrowing he always succeeds in achieving a unity of impression. This is because he does not slavishly imitate his sources but uses them for his own benefit. Obviously, he did not know the oral formulaic theory, but perhaps he instinctively knew that pillow words (*makura kotoba*) and other traditional devices characteristic of the *Man'yōshū* could be used with the same freedom as the fixed formulae of oral poetry.

Under these circumstances, it is not only difficult but also pointless to try to ascertain the exact degree of Ryōkan's indebtedness to individual poets of the *Man'yōshū*. Verbal echoes are found practically everywhere, but no poet or group of poets can be singled out as a leading inspiration. Yet to note the more conspicuous debts to these poets will be a useful basis from which to analyze Ryōkan's aesthetic preferences. What follows is a short list of such debts that I have found in the poems translated here. The first numbers refer to the poems in the present work, and the numbers in brackets refer to the poems in the *Man'yōshū* in which verbal echoes can be located.

Iwa no Hime: 369 (86)
Nukata no Ōkimi: 235 (9)
Kakinomoto no Hitomaro: 219 (196), 233 (239), 254 (3253), 324 2nd envoy (266), 390 (29, 199)
Ōtomo no Tabito: 263 (338)

Sakanoue no Iratsume: 247 (687), 250 (619)
Manzei: 380 (351)
Yamanoue no Okura: 218 (63), 244, 346 (892), 390 (803), 410 (1538), 413 (800)
Yamabe no Akahito: 405, 407 (317)
Yuhara no Ōkimi: 276, 277 (670), 308 (1550)
Tanabe no Sakimaro: 232 (1050)
Ōtomo no Yakamochi: 230 (3985), 233 1st envoy (1495), 313 (3911), 390 (478), 409 (994)

The list is far from being complete, but it is sufficient to show the wide range of influences coming from the *Man'yōshū*. The relative importance of Hitomaro, Okura, and Ōtomo no Yakamochi (716-785) should be noted—as should also the fact that they are among the greatest of the *Man'yō* poets. Ryōkan never succeeded in raising his personal sentiments to Hitomaro's level of epic grandeur, but he was interested in the elevated expression of feelings arising from deep within. Ryōkan could not forgive Okura for his rather self-righteous criticism of Buddhist monks, as he makes clear in one of his poems (413 in the text), but he appreciated the frank realism of Okura's style. Yakamochi was a bit of a dilettante and a littérateur, whose position Ryōkan could not accept because of his own ethical concern, but Ryōkan responded warmly to Yakamochi's ecstatic love of delicate and ephemeral beauty. It may well be that these are the reasons for the relative importance of the three poets, and the relative unimportance of Akahito may be explained on the ground that Ryōkan could not appreciate the descriptive purity of his poetic expression. It is dangerous, however, to carry these inferences too far, for the multiplicity of influences on Ryōkan indicates more than anything else the complexity and flexibility of his literary sensibility.

Ryōkan's indebtedness to the poets after the *Man'yōshū* has been pointed out by Yoshino Hideo (1902-1967) in his introduction to *Ryōkan Kashū* (Nihon Koten Zensho, Asahi Shinbunsha, 1952). According to his count, the number of Ryōkan's poems influenced by the respective anthologies and other traditional books is as follows:

Kiki Kayō 3, *Man'yōshū* 110, *Kokinshū* 66, *Gosenshū* 8, *Shūishū* 6, *Goshūishū* 5, *Shikashū* 1, *Senzaishū* 7, *Shinkokinshū* 22, *Shinchokusenshū* 5, *Zokukokinshū* 3, *Zokushūishū* 5, *Shingosenshū* 3, *Gyokuyōshū* 8, *Zokusenzaishū* 6, *Zokugoshūishū* 1, *Fūgashū* 1, *Shinsenzaishū* 4, *Shinshūishū* 3, *Shingoshūishū* 2, *Shinzokukokinshū* 2, *Shinyōshū* 1, *Kokinrokujō* 1, *Tsurayukishū* 1, *Sankashū* (Saigyō) 7, *Sanshōdōei* (Dōgen) 17, *Genji Monogatari* 2, *Ise Monogatari* 3,

Heike Monogatari 4, *Tsurezuregusa* 1, *Yōkyoku* (Noh plays) 1, *Bashō Bunshū* 1, *Goeika* (Buddhist psalms) 1, *Zokuka* (Popular songs) 4.

The listing shows that the influence of the poets after the *Man'yōshū* was considerable, and that the *Kokinshū*, *Shinkokinshū*, and the poems of Dōgen were the chief sources of inspiration. What follows is a list of the poems in the present selection in which I have been able to detect echoes from these three sources.

Kokinshū
 253 (349 Ariwara no Narihira), 283 (87 Ki no Tsurayuki), 285 (864 Anonymous), 289 (657 Ono no Komachi), 303 (334 Hitomaro), 307 (56 Sosei), 325 (202 Anonymous), 327 (983 Kisen), 331 (626 Ariwara no Motokata), 359 (165 Henjō), 362 (1060 Anonymous), 396 (970 Narihira), 403 (962 Narihira)

Shinkokinshū
 231 (262 Saigyō), 240 (64 Gyōkei), 245 (613 Fujiwara no Michinobu), 326 (290 Fujiwara no Hideyoshi, 268 Shokushi Naishinnō), 332 (342 Minamoto no Tsunenobu), 349 (618 Jien), 377 (7 Saigyō), 397 (1176 Fujiwara no Kiyotada), 402 2nd envoy (625 Saigyō)

Dōgen
 287, 307

In connection with the *Kokinshū*, it must be observed that Ryōkan's preference lay, not with the generation of the compilers of this anthology, but with the earlier poets, especially Ariwara no Narihira (825-880) who was criticized by Ki no Tsurayuki (868-945) for having "too much heart and too few words." The later poets appreciated technical excellence and worked for the establishment of a courtly diction, somewhat similar to the diction of Elizabethan poetry in its emphasis on elegant witticism, delicate description, meandering syntax, and rhythmic harmony. Mabuchi criticized these poets for using a feminine style (*taoyameburi*), but Ryōkan himself did not hesitate to use courtly diction. In 225, for example, he employed the techniques of the *kakekotoba* (pivot word) and of *engo* (word association) when he used the word *nagisa* both in the double sense of "beach" and "embalm" and in close proximity to the word *ura* meaning "bay." Furthermore, Ryōkan's frequent use of the smooth rhythm of the 7-5 syllabic pattern (*shichigochō*) reveals his indebtedness to the major poets of the *Kokinshū*. Yet his preference for

Narihira indicates, I think, that Ryōkan was not completely at home in their poetic manner.

In connection with the *Shinkokinshū*, it must be observed that Ryōkan's greatest inspiration came not from Fujiwara no Shunzei (1114-1204) nor from Fujiwara no Teika (1162-1241) but from Saigyō (1118-1190), who was par excellence the poet of *sabi* (a sense of loneliness). Both Shunzei and Teika tried to maintain the courtly tradition against encroaching forces of barbarism. During the Edo period, their style was defended by Kada no Arimaro (1706-1751) and Motoori Norinaga (1730-1801) but attacked by other critics. For example, Kamo no Mabuchi (1697-1769) calls it the music of a dying nation (*bōkoku no on*), Ozawa Roan (1723-1801) calls it too affected (*takumi sugi*), and finally Fujiya Mitsue (1768-1823) criticizes it on the ground that it is too flowery (*hana ni sugu*). Yet Mitsue defends Saigyō's style as being natural and uncontrived (*yasuraka ni tsukurowazu*). Perhaps it is this aspect of Saigyō that attracted Ryōkan. Moreover, Saigyō is reported to have said that he wrote poetry in the full realization that every natural object was in essence void and illusory (*kyomō*). As a Buddhist monk who renounced the world, Ryōkan had, I am sure, little difficulty in understanding this proposition. It is quite possible, I think, that when Ryōkan says in one of his Chinese poems (79) that his poetry is not poetry, he is expressing his sympathy with Saigyō's view. Here again, however, we must be careful not to carry the comparison too far, for, being a poet of the Edo period, Ryōkan had to make a greater compromise between the world and himself; consequently there is more of earthiness and humanity in his poetry than in Saigyō's. However, Ryōkan's frequent employment of the techniques of *honkadori* (echoing imitation) and *taigendome* (the noun ending) indicates that his indebtedness to the poets of the *Shinkokinshū* in general is greater than it seems at first.

I have been trying to construct a sketch map of the background of Ryōkan's *waka*. I must admit that the map still remains incomplete. For example, the use of *Kiki Kayō* (songs in mythological books) in 233, 4th envoy (*Kojiki* 111, *Nihonshoki* 85), in 274 (*Kojiki* 39, *Nihonshoki* 32), and in 408 (*Kojiki* 29, *Nihonshoki* 27); the use of the *Konjaku Monogatari* (V, 13) in 324, and of the *Heike Monogatari* in 364; and the frequent use of colloquialism should also be added. What the sketch map indicates is the immensity of Ryōkan's poetic background, which leads to the negation of his popular image as an amateur poet writing in total disregard of poetic tradition. On the other hand, the sketch map, however complete, cannot hope to show his real greatness as a poet, which lies, not in his use of tradition itself, but in his weaving of traditional materials into his own poetry. I should like to attempt, therefore, an analysis of some of his poems in order to show this shaping process.

No. 307 reads:

Hachi no ko ni / sumire tanpopo / kokimazete / miyo no hotoke ni / tatematsurite na.

> Purple violets
> In my broken begging bowl
> And dandelions
> Put together for contrast,
> I say prayers unto Buddha.

Here, *kokimazete* (put together for contrast) is an echo of the *Kokinshu* 56, where Sosei (fl. 905) describes the beauty of the capital city in its spring glory, especially the contrast of green willows and cherry blossoms. The echo, therefore, adds colour to the poem, arousing the memory of past glory; but Ryōkan is describing, not willows and cherries, but *sumire* (violets) and *tanpopo* (dandelions), humble flowers of the field. The first of these is a flower popular with the poets of the *Man'yōshū*, and although no specific reference is made here, we think, for example, of Akahito's poem about it (1424). Thus *sumire* functions as a kind of bridge to *tanpopo*. This flower is such a humble flower that it is not represented in any of the three major anthologies and, together with *hachinoko* (the broken begging bowl), comes from Ryōkan's daily experience. These seem to me the means by which his double response to the reality around him is expressed. He is aware of the sordidness of his daily life, epitomized by the broken begging bowl, but at the same time he knows that there is an element of beauty in it comparable almost to the past glory of the capital city. This ambivalent feeling is sublimated into a statement of pure faith when Ryōkan concludes the poem with a direct quotation from Dōgen (1200-1253). Dōgen's words are somewhat blunt, even harsh, in their original context, but here, placed side by side with the violets and dandelions, they gain fresh beauty and warmth.

Another poem of interest is 377:

Yamakage no / iwama o tsutau / kokemizu no / kasuka ni ware wa / sumiwataru kamo.

> Like the rivulet
> Running down in a trickle
> In a deep forest,

> I live here in quiet peace,
> Hidden away from the world.

Here, the image of "the rivulet running down in a trickle in a deep forest" comes, I think, from the *Shinkokinshū*, 7, where Saigyō discerns the arrival of spring in the almost inaudible sound of a long-frozen rivulet that has begun to melt; or possibly it may come from another poem usually assigned to Saigyō (as has been suggested by Yoshino Hideo in *Ryōkan Kashū*) where his cottage is described as smaller than the rivulet running down in a trickle. In any case, the echo of Saigyō is undeniable, and yet the obvious use of the technique of *joshi* (prefatory words preceding the main statement, often linked to it by similarity of sound or image) relates the poem primarily to the *Man'yōshū*. Again, no specific reference is made, but we think, for example, of 2855, where the word *sayaka* is used as a link between the prefatory words and the main statement, just as the word *kasuka* (note the similarity between the two words) is used by Ryōkan in exactly the same way. Furthermore, the use of the word *sumu* in the double sense of "to live" and "to clear" relates the poem to the *Kokinshū*, though somewhat vaguely in this instance, for *sumu* was a very popular *kakekotoba* (pivot word) also in the anthologies that followed. Basically, Ryōkan's aim in the poem is similar to Saigyō's: to describe the quiet solitude of his secluded life, but the poem gains descriptive freshness and psychological acuteness by its association with the *Man'yōshū*, and rhetorical richness by its association with the *Kokinshū*.

Another instance of a similar effect is 327:

Waga io wa / kimi ga urahata / yūsareba / magaki ni sudaku / mushi no koegoe.

> My grassy cottage
> Is at the back of your house,
>   Among dewy fields.
> Each evening by the hedgerow,
> An endless choir of crickets.

The way the poem opens reminds us strongly of that famous poem in the *Kokinshū* (983) in which Kisen (dates unknown) says, "My grassy cottage is on the melancholy hill of Uji, situated to the southeast of the capital city." Immediately after the opening, however, Ryōkan strikes his own note by using the humble image of dewy fields at the back of a house. The image is effective as a mild gibe at Kisen, whose melancholy is communicated to the reader as something not altogether pleasing. The gibe is so mild that the playful mood of Kisen's poem is not completely destroyed, but the use of a humble image convinces us that Ryōkan is more at home with the melancholy of his cottage. Ryōkan reinforces this impression by the description of crickets singing by the hedgerow. The use of the two expressions *yūsareba* (at the return of evening) and *sudaku* (swarm and sing in chorus) shows Ryōkan's indebtedness to the *Man'yōshū* in this part of the poem and gives it special freshness. Finally, the poem's conclusion is the typical noun ending (*taigendome*) of the *Shinkokinshū*, whose inconclusive ending is conducive to the creation of *yojō* (a suggestive quality). Thus the poem ends with the chorus of crickets and the endless reverberation it creates in the mind of the reader.

I think the three examples I have analyzed are sufficient to show how, within the short compass of the *waka* form, Ryōkan brings together elements from different anthologies and, by relating them to one another, weaves them into a poetic world of his own. We may often be misled by the surface simplicity of his poetry, but in most of his poems Ryōkan's complex sensibility is at work, selecting his materials from different levels of his experience and arranging them in such a way that they will express something that has never been said before. His response to his poetic sources is always subtle and flexible in that it is neither slavish imitation nor explicit rejection. In fact, it is acceptance and criticism combined. Few poets, I think, have succeeded in using such a wide range of poetic sources and giving the resulting work such a fine texture as Ryōkan. In my opinion, he must be granted one of the highest places in the literary history of Japan for this reason, if for no other.

At this point, I should like to turn to a discussion of Ryōkan's Chinese poetry. The position of *kanshi* (Chinese poetry) in the history of Japanese literature is a peculiar one. Never in the main stream, it has always been regarded as a genre existing in its own right, and as such exerted great influence on Japanese poetry. Three distinct periods of popularity for *kanshi* have been traditionally recognized. The first of these is the late Nara and early Heian period, when the impact of Chinese civilization was felt in virtually every aspect of Japanese life. Among the anthologies representing this period, the *Wakanrōeishū* is of special interest, for it is an attempt to bring together both *waka* and *kanshi* in one volume. Under the title of "March departing," for example, the following selections are included:

> I deplore my inability to retain the departing spring;
> Under the purple wisteria blossoms, twilight thickens.
> (Po Chü-i)

In sending spring away, we use neither cars nor boats;
Only, we say goodbye to the last warblers and flowers.
                              (Sugawara no Michizane)

    All beyond recall
    Cherry blossoms have scattered,
      So that my garden,
    Once the home of joyful spring,
    Looks now like an empty house.
                  (Ki no Tsurayuki)

As the example shows, Po Chü-i (772-846) was looked up to as a model during this period, and Japanese poets tried to emulate him in their attempt to combine emotion and wit. Even the rhetorical bias of the *Kokinshū* can be taken at least in part as a product of this literary tendency. Ryōkan was in the habit of writing both *waka* and *kanshi* on the same subject. This means, I think, that the spirit of the *Wakanrōeishū* was alive in his mind, but I have not been able to detect any direct influence, except in one instance (18) where he describes the fallen cherry blossom, using the expression *hana rōzeki* (havoc of flowers), which is found in a poem (129) by Ōe no Asatsuna (886-957). However, Ryōkan could have taken this expression from a Chinese poet, as I shall indicate later.

    The second period of popularity for *kanshi* comes in the Kamakura and Muromachi periods, when Zen monks brought fresh inspiration from China, and produced the literature of the so-called five temples (*gozan bungaku*). The following two examples will suffice to show their poetic style:

From a half-broken cobweb trails down a spider's thread;
A cherry blossom comes in a giddy flight, and is caught.
All day long, it keeps circling in the air without rest,
But elsewhere, the garden is quiet, not a wind stirring.
                              (Kokan Shiren)

The wind sounds hollow in lofty pines at a mountain temple;
The rain rustles a bamboo grove beside a riverside cottage.
There is no passage open here to the glory of worldly fame;
Quietly, a man regards plums and willows upon a log bridge.
                              (Ikkyū Sōjun)

Their style is characterized, I think, by *wabi* (sombre darkness) and *hie* (dry coldness). Instead of Po Chü-i, Su Shih (1036-1101), and Huang

T'ing-chien (1045-1105), together with Tu Fu (712-770), are said to have provided inspiration. Because of his Zen background, we would expect that Ryōkan came under the direct influence of these Zen monks, but I have not been able to discover anything beyond a general resemblance. This is partly because Ryōkan went directly to Chinese poets for inspiration, as I hope to show later, and partly because he could not blindly accept the sombre darkness of their style. Compared with them, Ryōkan often gives an impression of being less priestly.

The third and perhaps greatest period of popularity for *kanshi* is the Edo period, when the Tokugawa government adopted neo-Confucianism as its official philosophy, and encouraged the study of the Chinese classics. The establishment of public schools such as Shōheikō, as well as private ones, contributed greatly to the popularization of Chinese literature. The development of *kanshi* during this period is generally said to fall into three distinct phases. The earliest phase, represented by Fujiwara Seika (1561-1619) and Hayashi Razan (1583-1657), is somewhat barren of poetic achievements, and need not concern us here. The second phase, however, is of great importance, because it is characterized by a flowering of poetic talents. Ogyū Sorai (1666-1728) took the initiative when he maintained that in *kanshi* the "Great Poets" of the T'ang dynasty should be used as models (*Shi wa kanarazu seitō*), and the publication of Li P'an-lung's anthology of T'ang poetry by Hattori Nankaku (1683-1759) was an epoch-making event. The result was the creation of metrically perfect and, in choice of words, highly polished poetry. Here is an example by Nankaku himself:

> Jewelled screens, and silver dews, and shiny steps of the house,
> By the addition of the fireflies, gain special coolness tonight,
> For the tiny lights fly here and there in obedience to the wind,
> Some beyond garden trees, others slipping into ladies' chambers.

The reaction against this highly self-conscious poetry constitutes the third phase. Yamamoto Hokuzan (1752-1812) attacked it as a false imitation of T'ang poetry (*gitōshi*) and, following his lead, Kan Sazan (1748-1827), Rai San'yō (1780-1832), and many other poets began to write in a relatively free, unaffected style. Here is an example by San-yō:

> One night, at a riverside inn, I found the candle gloomy,
> And I heard what I thought was autumn rain dropping down,
> Yet opening my window, I discovered that it was not rain,
> But the stony river murmuring, shattering the lucid moon.

The contrast between the two poems is quite marked. Nankaku describes an imaginary situation with evocative language and imagery, whereas San'yō describes an immediate experience with a realistic touch.

Ryōkan himself began to write his *kanshi* just at the turn of the tide. A number of facts indicate that he was in sympathy with the new literary trend. First, he had among his friends the poet Kameda Hōsai (1752-1826), who severely attacked the imitators of T'ang poetry. Second, Ryōkan paid little attention to the rules of prosody. Suzuki Bundai (1796-1870) says of him, "Metrical rules are what my teacher disliked most (*shisei no ron, shi no mottomo yorokobazaru tokoro*)." Dainin (1781-1811) had to defend Ryōkan by saying that in spite of his metrical irregularities (*kikaku ni yorazu*), his poetry had the best music of all (*shidō chū no myōon*). Finally, most of Ryōkan's poems deal with an immediate experience, or at least start with one. Here again, however, we must be careful not to identify Ryōkan's position with that of the literary innovators of his time. In one of his Chinese poems (129), he points out that his poetic aim is to depict the scenes of his own heart. Thus, the kind of external realism we found in San'yō's poem is not Ryōkan's literary domain. He was always looking through his immediate experience to reach the inner depths of his mind.

Moreover, Ryōkan did not hesitate to learn from a wide range of Chinese poets. What follows is a list of verbal echoes I have found in Ryōkan's poetry. In preparing this list, I limited myself to the poets and poems included in the *Chūgoku Shijin Senshū* (First Series, Iwanami Shoten, 1957-1959), because the existence of a convenient index was a necessity. For each instance listed below, the first numbers refer to the translated poem by Ryōkan in the present work and to the line of the poem; and the numbers in parentheses refer to volume number (where necessary), page and line for the relevant poem in the *Chūgoku Shijin Senshū*. Thus, 132-1 (I-68-1) means that in poem No. 132, line 1, by Ryōkan in the present work, there is an echo from the *Chūgoku Shijin Senshū*, Volume I, p. 68, line 1 (of the poem, not necessarily of the page).

Shih Ching (Volumes I and II)
132-1 (I-68-1), 167-2 (I-158-4)

Ts'ao Chih (Volume III)
31-6 (89-6), 31-13 (45-9)

T'ao Yüan-ming (Volume IV)
12-8 (137-16), 49-12 (46-2), 63-7 (49-10), 74-5 (45-6), 76-1 (48-7), 97-10 (46-2)

Han-shan (Volume V)
   15-2 (113-2), 16-5, 6 (31-3, 4), 23-3 (113-3), 26-4 (113-4), 28-3 (50-6), 28-7 (50-7), 29-8 (55-8), 38-3, 4 (161-7, 8), 39-4, (46-6), 44-5, 6 (44-5, 6), 50-5, 6 (140-5, 6), 57-2, (25-6), 57-6 (129-2), 62-1 (166-1), 67-7 (40-8), 68-5, (82-6), 73-4 (50-2), 80-3 (46-6), 80-4 (93-7), 93-5, (189-1), 95-1 (143-1), 95-5, (126-7), 97-12 (82-6), 99-4 (128-8), 100-1 (129-1), 101-1 (40-8), 105-1 (170-1), 106-3 (91-8), 123-9, 10 (29-7, 8), 127-1 (170-1), 133-1 (105-1), 134-1 (88-1), 138-1 (62-7), 164-3 (113-2), 166-3 (26-8), 169-4 (25-6), 177-3 (132-7), 186-1, 2, 3, 4, (195-1, 2, 3, 4), 188-1 (93-1), 188-3, 4 (136-1, 2)

Wang Wei (Volume VI)
   14-3, 4 (122-4), 39-6 (126-6), 76-2 (109-1), 174-2 (81-3)

Li Po (Volumes VII and VIII)
   42-4 (VII-46-3), 64-5, 6 (VII-82-5, 6), 68-3 (VIII-129-4), 81-3 (VII-35-14)

Tu Fu (Volumes IX and X)
   49-2 (X-149-1), 49-3 (X-150-15), 51-27 (IX-21-7), 150-7 (IX-102-5), 178-11 (X-21-23)

Po Chü-i (Volumes XII and XIII)
   69-8 (XIII-42-10), 99-5 (XII-35-24), 178-24 (XIII-155-3)

Li Ho (Volume XIV)
   55-12 (69-1), 113-1, 2 (93-1)

Li Yü (Volume XVI)
   18-1, 169-1 (62-3)

The list is far from being complete: for example, Ryōkan's indebtedness to Han-shan (dates unknown) in 116-1, 2 and 118-1, 2, 3; to T'ao Yüan-ming (365-427) in 193-1, 2, 3, 4 and 200-4; to Chia Tao (777-841) in 16-8; and to Liu Tsung-yüan (773-819) in 15-1, 2 should be included among the important additions. Also, the possibility of alternative sources should be taken into account, for Ryōkan's apparent debt to Li Yü (937-978) may alternatively be a debt to Ōe no Asatsuna, as I have pointed out earlier. In spite of these limitations, however, the list can tell us some important things about Ryōkan's *kanshi*: first, Ryōkan's debts to Chinese poets, including the "Great Poets" of the T'ang dynasty, are very great; secondly, his debt to Han-shan is by far the greatest, and the spiritual congeniality of the two poets is not to be doubted; thirdly, T'ao Yüan-ming is the second most important poet in the list, and probably Ryōkan's debt to him is also more than accidental; fourthly, Wang Wei (699-761), Li Po (701-762) and Tu Fu (712-770) contributed more or less equally, whereas the contribution of Po Chü-i (772-846) was slighter; and finally, with the exception of a few instances, Ryōkan's borrowings do not extend beyond one or two lines, which indicates that his aim was not slavish imitation but free adaptation.

Ryōkan's indebtedness to Han-shan is so great, however, that it requires special attention. One of Ryōkan's Chinese poems (25) indicates that he had a copy of the works of this legendary hermit, and used it as a holy text (or prized it more highly than any holy text, as Han-shan himself recommended in one of his poems). In fact, the spiritual congeniality of the two poets was so great that Ryōkan found in Han-shan not only a poet to learn from but also a spiritual leader to follow, so that in many of his poems where direct echoes are not to be found, there is still an undertone which reveals his indebtedness to Han-shan. Roughly speaking, Han-shan's poetic domain can be divided into four areas: first, poems dealing with his secluded life, its utter solitude and poverty; second, philosophical poems in which he tries to understand himself through self-analysis; third, social poems, rather satirical in tone, in which he describes various evils to be found in the world; and finally, a small number of poems dealing with the nature of his own poetry. Ryōkan also wrote poems in each of these areas, and a comparison will be useful to show the degree of his indebtedness to Han-shan. Here is a poem by Han-shan on his life on Cold Mountain:

> Imprisoned at the foot of massive rocks I lie upon my back;
> Clouds and vapours constantly rise even during the daytime.
> My room is, therefore, gloomy, robbed of its natural light,
> And my heart is void of all the noise that the world makes.
> Dreams go their ways, visiting the golden gate of a temple.
> My spirit returns to that stone bridge high above a valley.
> I throw away everything that stands in the way of my peace,
> Like that dry gourd which made too much noise in the woods.

A comparable poem by Ryōkan is 44:

> Imprisoned by the walls of my hermitage I lie upon my back.
> For a whole day, not a soul comes to pay me a kindly visit.
> My begging bag hangs slack, with my bowl in its empty womb.
> My walking stick has surrendered itself to the piling dust.
> Dreams go their ways, revolving around the hills and moors.
> My spirit returns to the city where it once found pleasure.

At the busy street corners, I have not the slightest doubt,
Many boys are expecting me to return as a matter of course.

Ryōkan's indebtedness to Han-shan in this poem is very great. It goes beyond mere verbal echoes, for the whole structure of the two poems, and the view of life expressed in them, are similar. Yet the difference between the two poems is just as great as is their similarity. Han-shan's dreams go to the famous temple in the T'ien-t'ai mountain range, creating in the poem a profound sense of mystery. His last line contains a reference to Hsü Yu (dates unknown), one of the earliest of the Chinese legendary hermits, who is said to have thrown away even the dry gourd presented to him by a sympathetic friend as a substitute for a glass, as something unnecessary and cumbersome. The poem ends, therefore, with an overt expression of *contemptus mundi*. On the other hand, Ryōkan's dreams go to the hills and moors, recalling in the poem the memory of Bashō who, near death said that his dreams kept revolving around the moors. Moreover, Ryōkan's spirit returns to the street-corners where he often played with children. At first sight, this may look like an expression of Ryōkan's adherence to the world, but in the light of other poems we know that he found a supreme religious experience in the simple act of playing with children. Thus, Ryōkan's poem is no less an expression of mysticism than Han-shan's, and yet the emphasis is different. Han-shan finds mysticism away from the world; Ryōkan finds it within its boundaries. That is why we find in his poems more of the details of the world, especially of nature.

In his philosophical poems, we often find Han-shan making a self-caricature. "The Naked Worm" is the name he has given himself, and he often describes himself as a lunatic. In the following poem, we find him singing to the moon and dancing with the clouds:

Wise men of the world cast me away as a thing of no worth,
And as of no worth, I throw away foolish men of the world.
Being neither a fool nor a wise man in the ordinary sense,
I decline to have anything to do with the people at large.
At night, I sing loudly to myself under the luminous moon,
And I raid the morning, dancing with the gathering clouds.
How can I keep my mouth shut and my two hands firmly tied,
To be seated, a pitiful old man with his hair blown about?

A comparable poem by Ryōkan is 64:

Tatters, nothing but tatters, are the garments on my back,
And what else but tatters is left of my life, at this age?

> Seated on a wayside stone, I eat food given me in charity;
> I have long surrendered my house to the encroaching weeds.
> On a moonlit night, I sit up singing poems to my own ears;
> Led astray by the flowers, I roam away till I lose myself.
> Ever since I left the temple where I was once an inquirer,
> By my own sheer folly, I have sunk to this wretched state.

Here, Ryōkan's debt to Han-shan may not be so obvious as in the previous poem, but the fifth and sixth lines undoubtedly establish the connection. Yet what is a humorous description of lunacy in Han-shan becomes somewhat romanticized in Ryōkan, partly because his lines contain an echo of Li Po, perhaps the most romantic of the T'ang poets, and partly because there is a basic difference in the attitudes of the two poets toward themselves. Han-shan's self-caricature is a mask behind which his sharp criticism of the world and his confidence in his manner of life are hidden. Ryōkan, on the other hand, has a deep-rooted sense of guilt, and his lunatic singing and losing himself in the flowers are a romantic escape from it. Thus, Han-shan's self-caricature contains the voice of a man who has made a basic choice about life, and looks at himself with ironic placidity; Ryōkan's presentation of himself is characterized by a deeper involvement in the situation in which he finds himself.

I think these examples are sufficient to show Ryōkan's originality and greatness as a *kanshi* poet. Han-shan is perhaps more interesting philosophically, but Ryōkan is more interesting psychologically. If we compare their satirical poems, we will often find Ryōkan identifying himself with the object he is satirizing, but such emotional involvement is rare in Han-shan. If we compare their poems dealing with the nature of their own poetry, we will find Ryōkan showing a greater interest in the possibility of establishing rapport with his imaginary reader, as when he says in 79, "After you have learned my poetry is unworthy of its name, / I will sit down to discuss with you the secret of my art," or in 36, "Tomorrow, will I have voice to recite, given an audience?" In short, what makes Ryōkan unique as a writer of Chinese poetry is the profundity of the human experience that he expresses in a variety of tones. Ryōkan's *kanshi* can be dramatic, reflective, descriptive, or even sensual, but we always feel the omnipresence of a profound humanity.

Whether in *waka* or *kanshi*, what is most remarkable about Ryōkan is his openness to his poetic sources, combined with his ability to maintain his own poetic integrity. His poetry is the product of a mind that values its independence while remaining open to outside stimuli. This mental cast enabled Ryōkan to attain an unusual degree of subtlety in his poetry.

For this reason, his poetry presents numerous technical problems to a translator, but perhaps the greatest difficulty is the lack of any established practice in the presentation of the various Japanese and Chinese forms of poetry in translation. I do not think it advisable to use completely free lines, for that would destroy the delicate balance Ryōkan maintains between tradition and experiment, between freedom and restraint. In this translation, therefore, an attempt has been made to represent the visual solidity of the rectangular shapes of Chinese poetry by keeping the right-hand margins even (unless they are otherwise in the original) and also to keep the original syllable structure of Japanese poetry. In neither case is rhyme used, for I find that it clogs the movement. Although the result alone can justify my attempt, I have found the endeavour very rewarding. I think that the visual solidity contributes to the poetic solidity of the translations of Chinese poetry, and that the alternation of shorter and longer lines in the translations of Japanese poetry is most suitable for conveying the lyrical beauty of the *waka*. *Waka* are more formal than *haikai*, and I could not have translated them without attempting to give them some sort of fixed form.

The texts used for the translation are: Tōgō Toyoharu, *Zenshaku Ryōkan Shishū*, Sōgensha, Tōkyō, 1962 for the Chinese poems; Tōgō Toyoharu, *Ryōkan Kashū*, Sōgensha, Tōkyō, 1963 for the Japanese poems; and Ōtsuka Kasoku, *Ryōkan Zenshū*, Iwanami Shobō, Tōkyō, 1924 for *Dewdrops on a Lotus Leaf*. The parenthetical numbers at the head of the poems refer to these editions.

BIOGRAPHICAL SKETCH

WHERE A RANGE of wooded hills drops sharply into the Japan Sea, leaving a narrow strip of surf-tormented shore, there stand side by side the twin towns of Izumozaki and Amaze. These towns, situated some twenty miles to the south of Niigata City, were once important ports for the island of Sado, which was about thirty miles away and provided the largest single supply of gold during the Tokugawa period. In 1637, Izumozaki harboured 11 large coasters, 26 small coasters, 23 cod-fishers, and 182 skiffs; Amaze was the home of 26 large coasters, 30 small coasters, 2 cod-fishers, and 79 skiffs. The population of Izumozaki in 1781 was 2,601, and that of Amaze, 1,808. As these statistics indicate, the two towns were slightly different in character. Izumozaki was larger, and historically more important, but its prosperity depended to a considerable extent on the success of its fishing fleets. Amaze was smaller, and historically less well established, but it showed a clear bias toward the transport trade. They remained bitter rivals for many years, fighting to secure superiority in the lucrative government-supported transport business.

Ryōkan was born in Izumozaki in 1758, the first son of the headman of the town. According to the family records, which are no longer extant, his family was descended from Tachibana no Moroe, a famous courtier of the eighth century, and although the historical validity of this claim is difficult to establish, his household enjoyed the prominent name of Tachibanaya (House of Orange), although Yamamoto was the ordinary surname used by the members of the household. Ryōkan's father married into the Yamamoto family in 1754 from the nearby town of Yoita, to succeed his father-in-law as the headman of the town five years later. He was called Jirōzaemon Yasuo, but was better known to the world by his pen name, Inan. He was a distant disciple of Bashō and a friend of Kyōtai. Here are some specimens of his *hokku*.

> The plum blossoms gone,
> They look older than they are,
> Ancient cottage eaves.

> Taking on new forms,
> Summer clouds rise sluggishly,
> High above the hills.

2. Portrait of Ryōkan by Miyagawa Rokusai, painted in 1830

> At the single cry
> Of a bird, the startled moon
> Moves amid the reeds.

> All across the sky,
> A star has burned itself out,
> Above the cold sea.

As these examples indicate, Inan was an accomplished poet, good enough to be called after his death "the greatest among the restorers of the Bashō style in the north Etsu province." As headman, however, he was a failure. In 1761, for example, a quarrel broke out between him and another leader of the town, and he was accused of showing a despotic partiality in his handling of a public festival. In 1762, another quarrel broke out, this time between Inan and the headman of Amaze, concerning the construction of a new public notice-board in Amaze. Inan suffered a humiliating defeat in this quarrel, and he found it increasingly difficult to maintain the dignity of his household against the rising influence of his rivals. He retired rather unexpectedly in 1786. Of his tragic death in Kyōto, mention will be made later.

Ryōkan's mother, Hideko, was born in 1735 on the island of Sado, where her parents owned a wholesale business. She was adopted into the Yamamoto family by her adoptive father in 1751, three years before her marriage with Inan. Ryōkan's attachment to her was great, for after her death he wrote:

> Day in and day out,
> As my sweet mother's keepsake
> I love to behold
> The sea-bound isle of Sado,
> At daybreak and at twilight.

As a boy, Ryōkan seems to have exhibited some unusual traits. His early biographers have anecdotes, one of which relates that when his father said he would turn into a fish if he kept staring at him, he ran out to the beach and remained there till with some difficulty his mother persuaded him that it was not true. Other anecdotes tell us of his deep-rooted silence, his inability to cope with the affairs of the world, his habit of reading books as if addicted to them, and of the nickname given him, "a candle in the sun." These anecdotes, however, smack of exaggeration, and must not be taken as historical facts. That he was called Eizō as a boy, and that he looked back to his boyhood years with nostalgia, are established by the following poem:

> Should anyone inquire of me now what I think about myself,
> I would answer, I am just as I was in youth, Eizō by name.
>   (87)

Ryōkan received his basic education from Ōmori Shiyō, the Edo-trained Confucian scholar, who opened a school in the town of Jizōdō, some ten miles away from Izumozaki, and who taught the Chinese classics, especially Confucian ethics, to Ryōkan and his classmates. Ryōkan seems to have been a studious boy, for he wrote:

> As the thoughts of my boyhood return to me in this old age,
> I often picture myself reading a book alone in a huge hall.
> The burning candle before me has been replaced many a time.
> In those days I knew not the full length of a winter night.
>   (41)

It was at this school that Ryōkan developed his keen interest in literature, as he testifies in the following poem:

> When I was a boy, I had a couple of close friends about me.
> We often played together on the banks of the Narrow Stream.
> Already, literature was our concern, and we often sat down
> In an earnest conversation, not caring how time crept away.
>   (138)

We do not know how long Ryōkan studied at Shiyō's school, but long enough to qualify as a local administrator, and also to make a number of lifelong friends. Shiyō's school was closed in 1777 when the master departed for Tsuruoka in the North.

Ryōkan had three brothers and three sisters. Murako, born in 1760, became the wife of Toyama Shigeemon, and lived in the nearby town of Teradomari. Shinzaemon Yasunori, born in 1762, succeeded his father as the headman of Izumozaki. Like his father he proved to be a poor administrator, and he caused the downfall of his family, but he wrote *waka* under the pen name of Yūshi, and maintained close contact with Ryōkan throughout his life. Takako, born in 1769, lived in her native town as the wife of Takashima Iemon. Enchō (or Yūchō), born in 1770, became the head priest of the Enmeiji Temple in Izumozaki. Kaoru, the youngest of Ryōkan's brothers, established his fame as a scholar in Kyōto, but died at the age of 29. Mikako, born in 1777, married Sone Chigen, the head priest of Jōgenji Temple in Izumozaki, and later became a nun under the name of Myōgen. What is noteworthy about Ryōkan's brothers and sisters is that they all were interested in religion and literature. The following letter from Ryōkan to Yūshi will reveal the kind of relationship he maintained with his brothers and sisters.

> Yesterday, I received the ointment you had sent me. I think the messenger is responsible for the delay. Thank you also for the potatoes. I enjoyed them very much. I am perfectly happy at the moment, well supplied with everything I need.
> Not long ago, a salt jar was given me, which looks like this. (Drawing) It lacks a lid, and I think nothing would suit it better than the spiral shell of a turbo. Can you send me a few?—the larger the better, for they are hard to find here.
>
> > Under the heavens
> > What I crave at the moment
> > More than anything
> > Is some silver turbo shells
> > Lying far away on the beach.
> > (December 8)

What characterizes Ryōkan's letters is simplicity of diction and telegraphic shortness, but the presence of a warm humanity is felt behind his words.

As the first son of the family, Ryōkan was trained by his parents to become an administrator, but, contrary to general expectation, he renounced the world while he was still in his youth. We do not know exactly when he took the tonsure. Teishin, a nun who came to know him in his last years and compiled an anthology of his poems, *Dewdrops on a Lotus Leaf*, says in the introduction to her anthology that Ryōkan was twenty-two at the time; but in her manuscript, there is a correction which says he was eighteen, and it is difficult to know which is to be believed. As to the reasons for his becoming a monk, various conjectures have been made by his early biographers. Suzuki Chinzō, who knew Ryōkan as a friend, says, for example, that Ryōkan saw the execution of a robber, and that he renounced the world on the same day. Iizuka Hisatoshi has a different version in his *Tachibana Monogatari* written in 1843.

> In his youth, before he renounced the world, he was a great lover. He loved a woman so earnestly that he wanted her pledge of eternal love. One night, he went to her, but long before the first cockcrow, returned home, and straight away cut off his hair.

Oka Kamon, writing in 1888, has another version.

> Ryōkan became an official, following his father. One day a senior official advised him on how to mediate between the high and the low by saying he could maintain neutrality only by using a certain amount of cunning. In reply, Ryōkan said what he wanted was absolute truth and sincerity, and he became a monk, leaving his office to his brother.

Although each of these conjectures seems to have some basis in his poetry, it is probably wrong to assume that Ryōkan became a monk through the constraint of outward circumstances or through a Pauline conversion. It is more likely that his decision to become a monk was made slowly, and that it was a conscious act of choice rather than a case of being converted by a sudden revelation. Ryōkan himself is reported to have said, "Many a man becomes a monk and then practices Zen, but I had practised Zen for a long time before I became a monk."

Thus Ryōkan was studying Zen at the Kōshōji Temple in Amaze under Genjō Haryō in 1779 when Kokusen, abbot of the Entsūji Temple, came round on his lecture tour. Ryōkan must have found in him a great teacher, for he accompanied him all the way to Tamashima, and stayed at his temple till his master's death in 1791. Kokusen was born in the province of Musashi in 1718 and entered the Seiryōji Temple at Hikone at the age of thirteen. Judging from his calligraphy (see the certificate he gave Ryōkan), he must have been a man of unusual calibre. When he was asked about his principles, he is reported to have said, "I prize rolling stones and carrying dirt more than any principles." Under this teacher, Ryōkan studied Zen for more than ten years.

Ryōkan has a number of poems specifically dealing with his experiences at the Entsūji Temple. Tamashima is about 400 miles away from Izumozaki, and in this almost foreign environment he endeavoured to understand himself and the world about him. The following poem makes it clear that he tried hard to master "the art of quiet breathing."

> Many a time in my youth, I sat down for long meditation,
> Hoping to master by practice the art of quiet breathing.
> What virtue I now have in me to foster my heart's peace,
> I owe it to the hard discipline I underwent in my youth.
> (75)

In another poem, he speaks of the poverty he had to endure:

> Since I began to seek discipline at the temple, Entsūji,
> Many winters and springs have I known in abject poverty.
> All this is because I read in a chronicle of old saints
> That poverty was once prized by Sōka more than anything.
> (172)

Ryōkan's life at the Entsūji Temple, however, was not without moments of relief. One of his pleasures was drinking occasionally in the pine groves behind the temple, overlooking the Inland Sea with its tiny islands and shiny waters.

> On a hill behind the Entsūji Temple stands a shady forest.
> Drinking, I sat with you one summer day, to shun the heat.
> We emptied our cask to the last drop before we made poems.
> So protected, we sat there till the curfew closed the day.
> (174)

Another pleasure was the more ethereal one of watching his fellow-priests engaged in their respective activities. Nothing, I am certain, pleased Ryōkan better than the mutual harmony of his fellow-priests. It was heaven on this earth, but the priest that impressed him most was Senkei, whose duty was the humble one of growing vegetables:

> Priest Senkei is a sacred man, seeker after mysterious truth.
> Mute he works, his lips locked in silence.
> For thirty years, he has laboured under Priest Kokusen,
> Never sitting in a temple, nor reading holy texts,
> Not even saying a word of prayer in audible voice.
> Vegetables he grows, giving them free to the villagers.
> I saw him once, never seeing him in his true self,
> Met him once, never knowing him.
> Now I pine after him, hoping to follow him in my humble ways.
> Priest Senkei is a sacred man, seeker after mysterious truth.
> (165)

Thus at the end of ten years, Ryōkan had acquired sufficient knowledge and discipline for his teacher, Kokusen, to grant him a certificate in the form of a poem, and permission to establish himself as a Zen priest. The certificate reads as follows:

> To Ryōkan, good as foolish, who walks the broadest way
> So free and so untrammelled, none can truly fathom him,

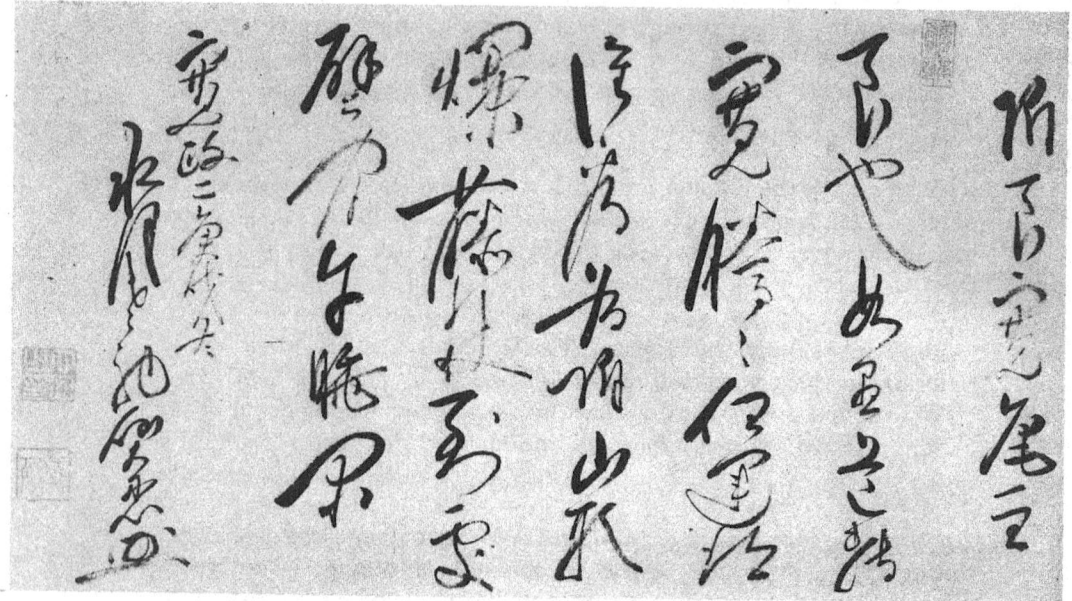

3. Certificate granted by the priest Kokusen to Ryōkan

I grant this certificate with a stick of mountain wood.
Everywhere he will find quiet rest as inside the walls.

The first line of the poem refers to Ryōkan's full name as a priest, Taigu Ryōkan, which literally means great-foolish good-broad. Not only this name, but also the poem itself, seems to reveal Kokusen's deep understanding of Ryōkan's nature. In fact it is possible to say that the last line is a prophecy of (or even a suggestion advising) Ryōkan's departure from the temple after Kokusen's death in 1791. We know that Ryōkan was not happy about the changes that took place at the Entsūji Temple, and that ever after his departure he regarded himself as a runaway.

Ryōkan seems to have spent the next few years wandering. Unfortunately, there is no reliable record to determine the course of his travelling. Kondō Manjō, native of Tamashima and poet of some fame in Edo, has left an account of his meeting with Ryōkan in southern Shikoku.

> When I was young, I travelled down to the province of Tosa. One day, rain and darkness descended on me about 7 miles outside the castle town. I found a lonely cottage about two hundred yards off the road. I went there, hoping to gain a night's

shelter. A priest with a pale, thin face was sitting by the fireside, and spoke not a word to me after the initial conversation. He was not in meditation, nor was he asleep. He uttered not a word of prayer. When I spoke to him, he only smiled to me, which led me to believe that he was slightly insane.

The cottage was empty, except for a wooden image by a window, and an arm rest with two books upon it. I opened the books to find that they contained the writings of Chuang-tzu, and a few poems inserted here and there in a beautiful, cursive script; no doubt, the priest's poems written by his own hand. Chinese poetry was not my line, but I was so impressed by his handwriting that I took out two blank fans and asked him to honour me with his writings. He depicted a spring warbler and a plum on one fan, and Mt. Fuji on the other. Although I do not remember the words he wrote, I do remember that the second fan decorated with Fuji was signed "Ryōkan, native of Echigo province."

This account is questionable on two grounds. First, the author used incorrect characters to spell Ryōkan's name, but this may be an innocent slip not uncommon in those days. Second, it is rather difficult to believe that Ryōkan, who left hardly any drawings, treated such common subjects as a warbler and a plum, and Mt. Fuji on the fans. Yet it is conceivable that he did so, being then in his early thirties. In any case, this is the only account that survives of the life of Ryōkan during the years of his wandering.

It seems probable that the five years Ryōkan spent in travelling were the darkest years of his life. Internally, he was going through the agonizing process of self-analysis in his attempt to determine the future course of his life. Externally, a number of incidents darkened his heart. In 1783, while Ryōkan was still at the Entsūji Temple, his mother died. Three years later, his father retired, and Yūshi succeeded him as the headman of Izumozaki. His father reached Kyōto in 1792, but three years later, for reasons which remain mysterious he jumped into the Katsura River and committed suicide. The cause of this tragic action has been variously conjectured. Issa ascribes it to an attack of beriberi, but others hold that it was a political protest to draw public attention to the ruinous state of the Imperial Court. Ryōkan must have heard this sad news while he was on the road, for he reached Kyōto in time for the memorial service for his father, held seventy-seven days after his death. Ryōkan also went to Kōyasan to pray for his repose. The following poem he wrote on his way to Kōyasan reveals the state of his mind in those days:

A bowl and a flask in my hand, I walk any distance, begging,
But what can I do in spring when my gown is torn to tatters?
I know full well I have not a single coin in my begging bag.
No doubt, I have erred, misled by the magic power of Nature.
(177)

Ryōkan seems to have spent a year or so, following his father's death, moving in and out of Kyōto, but in 1796 or thereabouts he made up his mind to return to his native place. What finally induced him to make this decision is not known, but he was already in his late thirties, and in poor health, as the following poem entitled "Sick at Itoigawa on a rainy day on my way home" testifies:

Nothing but a gown and a bowl on me, I have wandered long.
Here I am taken ill still on my road, and to nurse myself,
I sit by a window, one night, an incense burner before me.
The rain urges me to think about my ten years on the road.
(179)

From this point of view, Ryōkan's return to his native place was a kind of defeat on his part, or its acceptance, like the homecoming of a prodigal son, but that he had other reasons is seen from the following poem:

The red coral has its home on the floor of the south sea;
The purple lawn grows lush on the slopes of arctic hills.
Everything alive on earth has its home as its birthright,
Defined, not as it grows, but at the time of its genesis.
Having returned to where I belong, to a house by a cliff,
I gather early and late wild bracken sprouts for my fare.
(73)

From this point of view, Ryōkan's homecoming was a kind of destiny, a choice which once made looks inevitable. He must have felt that he had been drawn to his native place by an irresistible force, and that nowhere else he could enjoy that freedom which was necessary for the realization of his true self.

For about eight years from 1796 to 1804, however, Ryōkan had no permanent house to live in. Tachibana Konron has the following account of Ryōkan's homecoming in *Hokuetsu Kidan*:

There was an empty cottage at Gōmoto, right by the sea. One night, a priest came, and obtained permission to live in it. He begged in the nearby villages and satisfied his hunger. When he was given more food than he needed, he shared it with birds and animals. In half a year, villagers began to understand his rare virtue, and helped him with clothes, but he kept what was absolutely necessary, and gave the rest to the needy people he saw in the streets.

The cottage was only seven miles away from Izumozaki, and one villager thought of a possible connection with the priest and the house of Tachibana. My brother, Hikozan, went to identify him. The cottage was empty, its gate locked, not by a bar, but by overgrown vines. When he entered, my brother saw a desk with an ink slab on it and a fireplace with a clay pot hanging above it. The walls were covered with poems, which breathed forth a sweet breath of inspiration. By the style of calligraphy, my brother was able to identify the priest.

Again the historical validity of this account is questionable, but probably Ryōkan lived in very much the condition described above at least for a few years following his return to his native place. In 1797 Ryōkan was at Gogōan, the cottage where he eventually settled down, but in 1802 he was staying at the Mitsuzōin Temple at Teradomari and, in the following year, at the Saiseiji Temple at Nozumi.

This period of unsettled life in the vicinity of his native town must have been a sad one for Ryōkan from the worldly point of view, for he saw the increasingly rapid downfall of his household brought about by the misgovernment of his brother Yūshi. This family tragedy must be seen against the state of feudalism in those days. The Tokugawa government established in 1603 was nearly two hundred years old when Ryōkan returned home, and already signs of the weakening of feudalism were apparent everywhere. The ruling class of *samurai* found it increasingly difficult to cope with the rising power of the merchant class, and the policy of the central government oscillated between liberalism and extreme reactionism. When in 1772 Tanuma Okitsugu became the most influential member of the government he adopted the liberal line, furthering free economic and cultural activities. The result was aggravated inequality and a spread of luxury throughout the country. When in 1787 Matsudaira Sadanobu came to power he adopted a reactionary policy, by tightening the government control on economic and cultural activities. Now Yūshi, like his father Inan, was liberal in spirit, but he believed in the hereditary rights of his town and household. His opponent, the headman of Amaze, was perhaps less liberal in spirit, but he knew that the profits of his transport business were more dependable than his hereditary rights. Thus, when in 1800 Yūshi appealed to the central government for the protection of his hereditary rights, he was in fact approaching his problem from the wrong end, for the government had no ears to lend to the appeal of this obscure libertine. It was about this time, I believe, that Ryōkan wrote the following letter of admonition to him:

> Our bodies weaken after thirty or forty years of use. You must therefore watch your health. Heavy drinking and excessive lasciviousness are an axe that cuts into your life. You must learn to use your discretion. You can jump over a seven-foot screen, or tear the sleeves of close-woven silk, if you are so determined, as the proverb says. How can you not curb your natural desires, if you are so resolved?
>
> (undated)

In spite of this warning, Yūshi continued on his path, and in 1810 he was finally expelled from his town on charges of misappropriation of public money.

In 1804, Ryōkan was given permission to stay permanently at Gogōan, a cottage on the western slope of Mt. Kugami, a few hundred yards below the Kokujōji Temple. Kugami is a mountain of about a thousand feet in height, and the temple is situated halfway up the mountain, surrounded by a thick forest of huge pines and cedars, and overlooks a lovely vista of villages and rice fields. The temple was founded by Taichō in the Nara period, and its name appears in the *Konjaku Monogatari*, a collection of Buddhist tales compiled in the twelfth century, where in Volume 12 an interesting tale is told of how the founder overcame the thunder god by the power of a *sutra* to help build a tower of the temple and find an abundant supply of fresh water. As this tale indicates, the temple belongs to the Shingon sect, a branch of Buddhism that emphasizes the importance of esoteric rites and mysteries. Ryōkan's cottage itself is believed to have been built for Mangen, a guest priest of the temple, about a hundred years before Ryōkan moved into it, and it was named Gogōan (Five Bowls of Rice) from the fact that Mangen received five bowls of rice from the temple every day.

Ryōkan seems to have found at last the peaceful existence he had been looking for at this cottage. The poems he wrote here are permeated with a sense of deep satisfaction, mounting very often to a spiritual ecstasy. For example:

> My house is buried in the deepest recess of the forest.
> Every year, ivy vines grow longer than the year before.

Undisturbed by the affairs of the world I live at ease,
Woodmen's singing rarely reaching me through the trees.
While the sun stays in the sky, I mend my torn clothes,
And facing the moon, I read holy texts aloud to myself.
Let me drop a word of advice for believers of my faith.
To enjoy life's immensity, you do not need many things.
                                                    (24)

In another poem (62), he says that sitting under the roof of his grassy house, his conscience was perfectly clear. Living in this isolated environment, however, Ryōkan did not hesitate to receive occasional visitors, for, although he knew he was "suited by nature to seek pleasure by himself" (376), he had gained such maturity by this time that he no longer had to fly from the world. Two visitors who came from faraway places must be mentioned. First, there was Ōmura Mitsue, a poet and student of Kamo no Mabuchi, who visited Ryōkan from Edo and left the following account of his visit:

> I visited a man of rare virtue at Mt. Kugami. At his cottage, I wrote late at night:
>
> > Behind the low hill
> > Where we gathered anise twigs,
> >   Alas, the moon has set,
> > And the pine-wood door is dark.
> > Come, let us lie down to sleep.
>
> Early the following morning, when I was about to depart from his cottage, my host detained me with the following poem:
>
> > In the shady grove
> > Outside my pine-built cottage,
> > Rain began to fall, drizzling.
> >   My beloved friend,
> > You must stay here in my house
> > A while longer till it clears.
> >   (275)

There was also Kameda Hōsai (or Bōsai), a Confucian scholar, who closed his school in Edo in 1790 when the government tightened its control on cultural activities and banned unofficial schools of Confucian studies. Ryōkan welcomed him with the following poem, when he came to the province of Echigo as a wandering scholar.

> Hōsai is an extraordinary man, armed with a brave spirit.
> For reasons beyond my reach, he rambled out to this area.
> I came upon him yesterday amid the roar of a market city.
> Our hands cemented, we both choked ourselves in laughter.
> (158)

It is noteworthy that Ryōkan had a literary rebel like Hōsai among his friends, for it shows that he also had a rebellious spirit buried deep in his inner self, always thirsting for its absolute freedom.

During his stay at Gogōan, Ryōkan often went to the nearby towns and villages to beg. Begging was for him not only a means of obtaining a livelihood but also a holy act, and the misshapen begging bowl he carried in his hand was not a mere receptacle but the image of his whole existence—of his soul expressed in its circular shape, of his sins symbolized by its deformity, and of his faith shining in its polished lustre. That is why he said, when he lost it by mistake, that he had to search it out at all costs, and that it was a great pity that no one cared enough to steal it. The same can be said about the silk ball he carried in his sleeve and bounced with children on his begging rounds. He wrote of it:

> The silk ball in my sleeve pocket is worth my soul.
> The best bouncer, proudly, is no other than myself.
> Should anyone question me on the secret of the art,
> By way of reply: one two three four five six seven.
> (6)

The image of Ryōkan as an old priest with a bouncing ball has been so popularized that the profound religious meaning Ryōkan attached to the simple act of bouncing a ball with children is often overlooked; but it was for him the highest form of Zen. In this poem, therefore, the natural sequence of numbers in the last line is an expression of his ideal of perfect proportion and harmony, which is not only aesthetically pleasing but also religiously inspiring.

In 1816, Ryōkan left Gogōan after a twelve-year stay, and began to live in a cottage by the Otogo shrine at the foot of Mt. Kugami. He was already in his late fifties at the time, and probably found it easier to live closer to the villages than halfway up the steep slope of Mt. Kugami. The Otogo shrine is dedicated to Takemorosumi no Mikoto, the youngest son (*otogo*) of Ame no Kagoyama no Mikoto, who is enshrined in a larger shrine some three miles to the north at the foot of Mt. Yahiko. Of the Otogo shrine, Ryōkan has written:

> Foothills far below
> Mount Kugami soars to heaven.
> At its shady foot
> Stands the shrine of Otogo.
> Here I live alone,
> Every morning and each night,
> On the rugged rocks,
> Or through the mossy footway,
> Coming and going
> To perform my daily chores.
> Before me rises,
> Each time I cast up my eyes,
> A primeval grove,
> Divine in its dark grandeur.
> Every year in May,
> Cuckoos return from the south,
> And in noisy flocks,
> Swell their throats in ecstasy.
> When, in September,
> Rain comes drizzling from above,
> Seated by the hearth,
> I tear off bright maple leaves.
> Thus for many years,
> As long as life stays with me,
> Here I shall live free as air.
> (233)

In this environment, Ryōkan lived for ten years, "not unlike a shrine keeper, or unlike a prophet of Buddha." This rather enigmatic line of his Chinese poem (88) indicates, I think, the persistence of his sense of guilt, but there is little bitterness in the tone of his voice.

The descent to the Otogo shrine seems to have enabled Ryōkan to have closer contact with his friends in the villages. Judging from the number of extant letters he wrote to each of his friends, the following names should be remembered. First, we have Abe Sadayoshi, the village head of Watanabe, to whom Ryōkan wrote by far the largest number of letters (forty-seven are extant). He was a student of Ōmura Mitsue, and not only helped Ryōkan with food and clothes, but also exchanged poems with him, as the following letter testifies:

> Thank you for the bottle of holy *sake* you sent me yesterday. I enjoyed reading your poem on the New Year. Here is my reply:

>   Under the heavens,
>   At the commencement of this
>   Felicitous year,
>   Who can be so ill-natured
>   As not to express his joy?
>   (undated)

Next we have Kera Shukumon, the village head of Maki ga Hana, who seems to have invited Ryōkan to his house many times, as the following letter reveals:

> Thank you for your letter which reached me this morning. I returned to my cottage only the day before yesterday, and I have not yet begun my preparations for the winter. When things are a little more under control, I shall pay you a visit. I live alone in the mountains, yet I am not free. It is quite understandable that all the people of the world should be busy all the time.
>
>   Whatever I do,
>   I do not ply my own trade
>   Or my business,
>   Yet I have but a few days
>   I can spend in quiet peace.
>
> I must thank you for the towels and the late chrysanthemum you sent me.
>   (October 5)

Of the letters Ryōkan wrote to Kera Shukumon, twenty-one are extant, and his son, Yoshishige, wrote *Ryōkan Zenji Kiwa* in which some important testimonies about Ryōkan's poetic doctrine are to be found, as I mentioned in the introduction.

Next, we have Yamada Tokō, a sake brewer of Yoita, who had a keen interest in *haikai*. Of the letters Ryōkan wrote to him, thirteen are extant. Here is a famous one about the earthquake that took place in 1828:

> The earthquake was a big disaster, but nothing happened at my cottage. It was a relief to know that no one was killed among your relatives.
>
>   Far better it were
>   To surrender my whole life
>   Than abide so long,

> So long indeed as to watch
> Such a blight come upon us.

However, when a disaster comes, we must go through it, just as when death comes we will be better off by going through it. This is the only way to escape real disaster.
                                                      (December 8)

The prevailing atmosphere of Tokō's house, however, was a joyful one. One letter makes it clear that Ryōkan was nicknamed "Crow" on one occasion at this house, and in another letter, he sent a request for *sake* in the name of a thirsty firefly.

Among other friends, mention must be made of Harada Arinori (Jakusai), a doctor and classmate celebrated by Ryōkan as a flower-thief; of the Suzuki brothers, Ryūzō and Chinzō, both doctors and scholars at Yoshida, from whom Ryōkan obtained medicine and with whom he discussed Li Po and Tu Fu; of Miwa Gonpei, a rich merchant in Yoita who lent Ryōkan Chikage's commentary on the *Man'yōshū*; and, finally, of Miwa Saichi and his niece, Ikei, both of whom looked up to Ryōkan as a religious teacher. Surrounded by these friends, Ryōkan's life at the cottage by the Otogo shrine must have been a relatively happy one, but already, age was weighing heavily on him, as the following poem testifies:

> For sixty years and more I have been but an ailing priest.
> My cottage is beside a shrine, away from the smoking town.
> Late at night, rains flood down, rooting up massive rocks.
> Before my dark window the candlelight falters in the wind.
>   (90)

In 1826, Ryōkan left the cottage by the Otogo shrine after a stay of ten years, and moved to a small hut attached to the house of Kimura Motoemon in the town of Shimazaki. This was a move necessitated by his age. Earlier in the same year, a man named Genzaemon had asked if Ryōkan would let him build the poet a new cottage in his village, but on that occasion Ryōkan had firmly declined the offer, by saying that he would not like a new house. When he was invited by Kimura Motoemon, however, Ryōkan said neither yes nor no, but gave a silent consent. In the letter he wrote to Abe Sadayoshi at the end of 1826, Ryōkan complains of the smallness of his hut:

> I am staying in a hut attached to the house called Notoya in Shimazaki this winter. It is so small that I feel uncomfortable. I

shall probably go to another place when the warm weather comes. Thank you for the *sake*, tobacco and vegetables you sent me.

(December 25)

Ryōkan's complaints about the size of the hut came partly from psychological reasons. Living so close to the villagers, he seems to have been dragged into their affairs much against his will. Kimura Motoemon was kind to him, no doubt, but often Ryōkan found his kindness too patronizing. In a letter to his friend, Motoemon is reported to have said, "With a famous master like Ryōkan under my roof, I feel as if I were a fox wearing a tiger skin." A comment like this was embarrassing to Ryōkan, for he believed that all his life he had "laboured to draw a tiger, painting but a cat (87)." Moreover, Motoemon was a devout follower of Shinran, founder of the Jōdo Shinshū sect, who preached salvation through earnest prayers. It is conceivable, I think, that there was in Ryōkan's mind a tension between the teachings of Shinran and the earlier Zen background.

The happiest event in Ryōkan's final years was his encounter with Teishin, a nun who became his disciple in religion and literature, and collected his *waka* in an anthology named *Dewdrops on a Lotus Leaf*. She was born in 1798, a daughter of Okumura Gohei, a minor *samurai* in the service of the feudal lord of Nagaoka. She married a country doctor named Seki Chōun at seventeen, but the marriage ended five years later with her husband's death, and soon after this, she took the tonsure and became a nun. She was living in a small temple called Emmadō in the village of Fukushima not far from her native place when she visited Ryōkan at Shimazaki for the first time in 1827. She was twenty-nine and Ryōkan was sixty-nine at the time. Since Teishin had written to the wife of Kimura Motoemon in advance, she was fully informed of Ryōkan and his life when she came to visit him. Yet their first meeting was an encounter in the true sense of the word—a violent coming together of two kindred souls across time and space. For Teishin, it was a dream come true, as the following poem testifies:

> Having met you thus
> For the first time in my life,
>   I still cannot help
> Thinking it but a sweet dream
> Lasting yet in my dark heart.

For Ryōkan, it was finding a ray of hope in the death-benighted final stretch of his life. His reply to the above poem was:

BIOGRAPHICAL SKETCH

> In the dreamy world,
> Dreaming, we talk about dreams.
> Thus we seldom know
> Which is, and is not, dreaming.
> Let us, then, dream as we must.

Thus for five years till his death, Ryōkan and Teishin met occasionally and exchanged poems. In my opinion, whether feelings of love actually existed between them or not is a matter of little importance. The poems exchanged between them are of the quality of the best love poems of the classical period.

In 1830, Ryōkan became seriously ill. We do not know the exact nature of his illness, but he suffered from continuous diarrhoea. About this experience, he wrote as follows:

> Upon the dark night,
> When will the dawn come to smile?
> Upon the dark night,
> If the pied dawn starts to smile,
> A woman will come
> And wash my foul garments clean.
> Rolling many times,
> I fouled my shirts and my pants,
> Aching through the entire night.
> (249)

When his brother Yūshi visited him on his death-bed on December 25, Ryōkan had still strength enough to exchange poems with him, but when Teishin arrived at the end of the year he had only a few more days to live. An account of his death is given by her in *Dewdrops on a Lotus Leaf*.

> He grew weaker and weaker, and it was obvious even to me that he had only a few more days to live:
>
> > To life or to death
> > I should cast a cloudless eye,
> > Faithful to our vow.
> > Yet at this last leave-taking,
> > How can I restrain my tears?
>
> By way of reply, my master recited to me the following lines in a low voice:

> Maple leaves scatter
> At one moment gleaming bright,
> Darkened at the next.

Ryōkan died on January 6, 1831, and to his funeral service held two days later many villagers came with small obituary gifts, such as candles, rice-cakes, and vegetables. He was buried at the Ryūsenji Temple, not far from the house of Kimura Motoemon in Shimazaki.

Ryōkan is often given various labels, such as eccentric, revolutionary, ascetic, fool, beggar, but he defies all such simple names. Certainly, he was an eccentric to the extent that many anecdotes grew up about him, but he was never against the use of reason, and perhaps his sanity and common sense are best expressed in the few letters of admonition he left behind. He was a revolutionary in the sense that he had a rebellious spirit that hated any form of external restriction, but at the same time he valued obedience and devotion just as much as freedom. He knew life was a series of choices, but he also knew that choices ought to be made in the direction of greater harmony. He was an ascetic and sustained his flesh with "simple tea and plain rice," but he was human enough to admit that "severe fasting is detrimental to health," and that "ill health is likely to breed ill thoughts." He was a fool in a sense, and even children used to make fun of him, but his foolishness was an expression of his great wisdom, and his meaning, "ampler than words," was always addressing itself to people about him. He was a beggar, beyond any doubt, and spent most of his life in abject poverty, but he was an aristocrat on the spiritual level. Walking from house to house, begging for alms, he rose "far beyond the glory of the rich emperor." In short, Ryōkan was a great man who lived above all definitions, firmly refusing to see life in slices, faithful to that whole truth where contradictions cease to be contradictions, yielding to a harmonious unity. Ryōkan is often called a Zen priest, and no doubt he was, but somehow even this definition seems to be too limited to embrace the greatness of this man. He was, in fact, undefinable, like "the great wind above heaven," which he himself took as a model for his life.

Chinese Poems

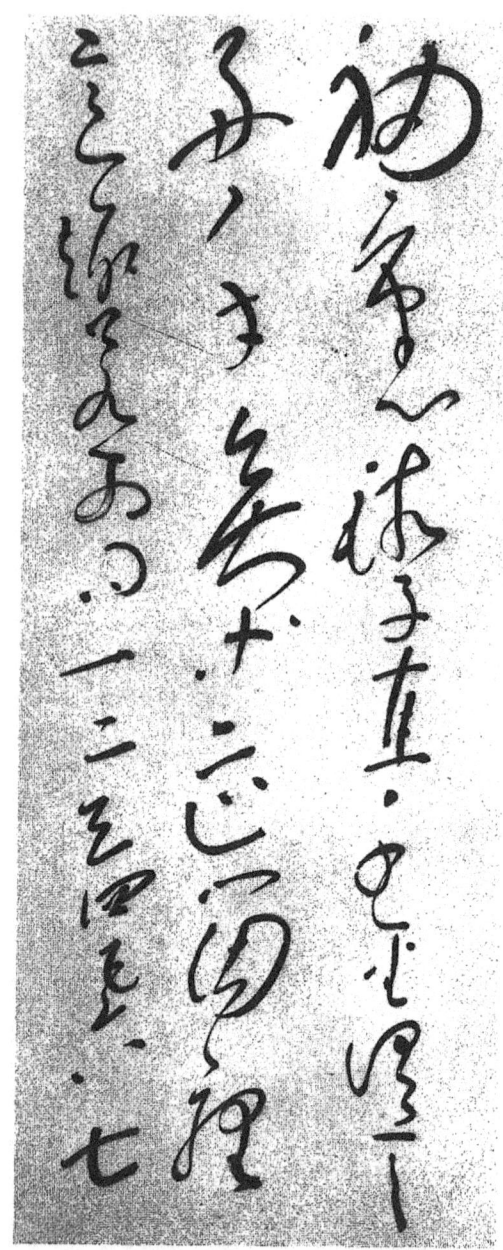

4. Chinese poem by Ryōkan (No. 6)

CHINESE POEMS

1.   At crossroads and through streets I begged all day.
(1)   My wandering steps have led me to a village shrine.
       Children come around me, whispering one to another,
       The silly priest of last year has returned to play.

2.   My walking skirt is short, but my holy gown is long.
(2)   Enraptured, I work for hours my own flesh and bones.
       Children stop me in a street, and sing loudly to me
       A bouncing-ball ballad, beating their hands for joy.

3.   Once I sought to triumph at a grass-fighting game.
(3)   I revelled in beating children, one after another,
       Till evening closed, and I was left alone to view
       A perfect moon ascending the cloudless autumn sky.

4.   My hair over my ears and my ears big enough for note,
(4)   My garments are torn to tatters like shredded clouds.
       Half-awake, half-asleep, I trudge along towards home.
       Children escort me, some ahead of me, some behind me.

5.   Day after day, yet at the return of another long day,
(5)   I take pleasure in playing with the village children.
       In my sleeves I always have hid a few bouncing balls.
       Incompetent otherwise, I luxuriate in spring delight.

6.   The silk ball in my sleeve pocket is worth my soul.
(6)   Its best bouncer, proudly, is no other than myself.
       Should anyone question me on the secret of the art,
       By way of reply: one two three four five six seven.

7.   All day long I walk through streets, begging for food.
(8)   At night I sit for meditation below a protruding rock.

Nought else have I but a holy gown and a begging bowl.
This practice as a soft wind from the west I venerate.

8.   Early, on August the first,
(10) I set out to beg in a city.
Silver clouds sail with me.
Golden winds ring my bells.
At dawn I see the thousand gates and doors thrown open.
At noon I feed my eyes with cool bamboo and bashō tree.
East or west, I will not pass a single house unvisited,
Not even the slimy haunts of drunkards and fishmongers.
Straight glances of honest eyes break a pile of swords.
Strides of steady feet scorn the heat of boiling water.
Long ago the Prince of Pure Eating preached how to beg,
And the Beggar of Beggars truly acted out his teaching.
Since then it is two thousand, seven hundred years and more.
Yet am I no less a faithful pupil of the First Teacher.
Therefore I beg, a bowl in my hands, a gown on my back.
Have you not read or heard
Of that noble man of high repute, who solemnly decreed,
Equal in eating, equal under the divine law we must be.
Look out, everyone, lest you should run loose unawares.
Who stands secure against the lapse of countless years?

9.   Begging on the road, I was caught by a sudden storm.
(11) Directly I sought shelter in an aged village shrine.
Laugh, whoever is tempted, at my sad bowl and flask.
Reconciled am I to finding myself in a ruined house.

10. A few chrysanthemums still about the darkening hedge,
(14) Wintry crows wheel above the cluster of silent trees.
Distant hills and mountain crests aglow with the sun,
Time for me, perhaps, to embrace my bowl and go home.

11.　In springtime, all the airs seem to stay in harmony.
(15)　Ringing my bells, I walk out to the city's east end.
　　　In a garden, willow trees are sprouting fresh green,
　　　And water weeds lie afloat on a sleepy lake surface.
　　　My begging bowl is loaded with a heap of white rice,
　　　And I rise far beyond the glory of the rich emperor.
　　　Hoping truly to follow upon the heels of holy sages
　　　I march along from house to house, begging for alms.

12.　All the day long, I have begged most unsuccessfully.
(20)　From village to village, I dragged my worn-out feet.
　　　At sunset, I have many more mountainous miles to go.
　　　The wind is strong enough to split my beard asunder.
　　　My garments are reduced to shreds of thinning smoke.
　　　My empty bowl, discoloured from use, looks deformed.
　　　Such as I am, I will not grudge, nor spare my pains.
　　　Cold or hungry, go I must as many a saint before me.

13.　This rank absurdity of mine, when can I throw it away?
(22)　This abject poverty I shall take to the grave with me.
　　　After dark, along the dirt road of a decaying village,
　　　I carry homeward my begging bowl, weathered and empty.

14.　After a long day of begging in the city, I go homeward,
(23)　Fully contented with what I have got in my begging bag.
　　　Holy man, which way lies your home, your resting place?
　　　Somewhere beneath those clouds, is all I know about it.

15.　Frozen snow holds all the mountain tops about my house.
(25)　Barred from human approach, footways of the valley lie.
　　　Day after day, I sit by myself facing the wall of clay.
　　　I hear now and then snowflakes brush against my window.

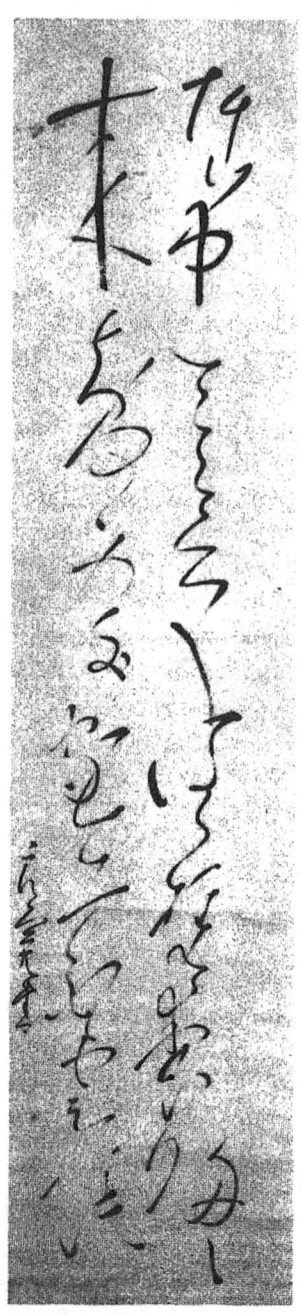

5. Chinese poem by Ryōkan (No. 14)

16. My hermitage is named after the Five Bowls of Rice.
(26) My room is naked, except for the gong, as they say.
     A thousand cedars stand together outside my window.
     A few odes in my saviour's praise hang on the wall.
     An iron pot, my rice-cooker, has some kitchen dust.
     My hollow furnace is seldom heated by cooking-fire.
     Yet in an east village I have a friend, an old man.
     He often knocks at my gate beneath the bright moon.

17. Bent under a pile of firewood, I walk down a hill.
(27) The green hill road is too steep for my aged legs.
     I take a moment's breath, beneath a towering pine.
     With a quiet mind, I hear spring warblers twitter.

18. On the garden steps, gay havoc made of cherry flowers.
(28) The sweet colloquy of birds spreading like a tapestry.
     Slow steps of the sun loitering a while at the window,
     Pale smoke ascends undisturbed from an incense burner.

19. The cottage gate remains unlocked most of the year.
(29) Seldom do callers stir the deep quiet of my garden.
     Today, after the prolonged rain of the plum season,
     Myriad oak leaves lie scattered on the mossy earth.

20. The bashō tree spreading its big leaves at my window
(30) Climbs upwards, all but tall enough to brush the sky.
     Beneath its cool shade, I make poems, long and short,
     Not for a moment leaving this quiet seat by the tree.

21. Where can I cover myself from the summer heat, except
(31) Here, this place of self-exile, the Shrine of Izuruta,
     Where the chorus of cicadas supplies music to my ears,
     And the surrounding woods, unasked, breathe fresh air?

22.   Utterly devoid of movement, this small house of mine,
(32) All day long, not a single human eye ever glances in.
       I sit alone at the window, absorbed in deep thinking,
       My ears bent to the quiet falls of scattering leaves.

23.   Already well-advanced in hours, this late-autumn night.
(33) Cold dewdrops have penetrated through my outer garment.
       Darkness has rendered invisible the walls of my garden.
       Crickets singing underneath dying grass are all I hear.

24.   My house is buried in the deepest recess of the forest.
(34) Every year, ivy vines grow longer than the year before.
       Undisturbed by the affairs of the world I live at ease,
       Woodmen's singing rarely reaching me through the trees.
       While the sun stays in the sky, I mend my torn clothes
       And, facing the moon, I read holy texts aloud to myself.
       Let me drop a word of advice for believers of my faith.
       To enjoy life's immensity, you do not need many things.

25.   To the end of the day I walked along, begging for food.
(35) Having reached home, I close behind me my cottage door.
       Then I build a fire with branches still bearing leaves,
       And read quietly poems of Kanzan, a hermit of old days,
       While the swelling west wind brings with it heavy rain.
       My thatched roof moans under the weight of the tempest.
       But my legs stretched at ease, I lie down on the floor.
       What have I to worry me, or to raise doubt in my heart?

26.   Since I began to climb this steep path of discipline,
(36) I have lived behind a fast gate and a thousand hills.
       Aged trees rise dark about me, fettered by ivy vines.
       Rocks look cold on hillsides, half-covered in clouds.
       The posts of my house are all ruined by nightly rain,
       My holy gown reduced to shreds by early morning mist.
       No news of me my kin or the world have cared to know,
       Year after year, for all the years I have lived here.

27.
(40)
As a summer night advances into chaste hours of morning,
From bamboo leaves, dewdrops fall to the brushwood gate.
The pounding noise from my west neighbour has long died.
The rank grass of my garden is moist with gathering dew.
Far and near, the frogs of the marsh chant their chorus.
High and low, fireflies fly about, their lamps blinking.
Keenly awake, I cannot possibly seal my eyes with sleep.
Slowly rubbing my pillow, I think beyond time and space.

28.
(41)
A solitary trail stretches away through a million trees.
A thousand pinnacles above me are hid in cloud and mist.
Not autumn yet, fallen leaves lie thick upon the ground.
Hardly a rainy day, but all the rocks are dark and grim.
A basket in my hands, I hunt for mushrooms in the woods.
A bucket below my arm, I draw water from a stony spring.
Who can indeed content himself with this manner of life,
Unless he has seen himself altogether lost in the world?

29.
(44)
I sit down and shut my eyes, as darkness dims the hills.
The thoughts of human affairs leave me, creating a void.
Unable to sustain myself, I lean against the bedclothes
And, half-awake, look into the blank void of the window.
The smoke of the incense burner has measured itself out.
Dewy as it is, I am naked, with but a thin gown upon me.
Rising from my meditation, I stroll about in the garden,
Whence I see the clear moon rise above the highest peak.

30.
(48)
I am imprisoned in my cottage among the solitary hills,
And think about the wet snow driving outside my window.
The cries of black monkeys are echoed by rocky summits.
The icy stream runs hushed at the bottom of the valley.
The flaming light by the window is chilled to its core,
And frost-dry is the ink slab I have placed on my desk.
The night has thus prevented me from falling to repose.
I employ my brush, often warming it with my own breath.

31. On the floor of an empty hall I planted myself alone.
(51) But nowhere could I find ease for my oppressed heart.
And so I mounted a horse, travelling far at a gallop,
And climbed a mountain, to command a vast, vast view.
Presently a whirlwind came blowing out of the ground,
And the sun dropped westward, losing its usual light.
The winding river at once surged, its waves mounting,
And the boundless stretch of wilderness lay obscured.
Black monkeys called one another in descending gloom,
And a stray fowl roved southward, flapping its wings.
When I saw this, a hundred thoughts twisted my brows,
And fear a million times sterner froze my inner core.
Groping for a way to retreat, I could nowhere see it.
Like the year at its close, I stood lost unto myself.

32. Among the low foothills of Mt. Kugami, I have my home,
(54) And with simple tea and plain rice I sustain my flesh.
Long have I hoped to receive a guest with spiked ears.
But men gathering dry firewood are all I can see here.

33. Upon the top of Mt. Kugami, I once turned my head to see
(55) The heavy frozen sky and the dying sun at its lowest rim.
The day before, I had gathered some nuts and drawn water.
Those woods and that spring now below the obscuring blue.

34. A burglar made away with my leaning block and my cushion,
(60) But who could have hindered him from entering my cottage?
On the night I was robbed, I sat down at my black window.
Passing showers made empty sounds in the bamboo thickets.

35. O, the woeful state of this world and man's frozen heart!
(61) I know not where under heaven I can find my life's peace.
Yesterday night, beating drums were heard in the village.
Alarm, they say, at a thief's approach, to scare him off!

36. In sickbed I remain awake, my eyes under a strange spell.
(63) All the walls about me are dead silent, as night deepens.
     The candle remains flameless, the fireplace without heat.
     Icy cold creeps, unprevented, beneath my pillow and gown.
     Having nothing else to comfort me, I rise out of the bed,
     And leaning on my crooked cane, I stagger into my garden.
     On the twigs of leafless trees I see stars in full bloom,
     And a distant stream plucks a cordless harp, as it falls.
     Tonight, I have had the bare strength to write this poem.
     Tomorrow, will I have voice to recite, given an audience?

37. My walking stick and straw sandals in this swampy village
(64) Have lured me out to enjoy an easterly breeze in February.
     Spring warblers are now in the bush, learning their songs.
     Strips of snow about the hedge, grasses already sprouting.
     I met a friend by the way, and we spoke of grave subjects.
     We opened books at his house; heads in our hands, thought.
     A perfect evening, both lights and winds in quiet harmony,
     A plum tree breathing sweet inspiration to my blest heart.

38. I have in my possession an old cane to support my weight.
(65) From whom it came to me, what history it has, I know not.
     From long use, the bark has dropped away, layer by layer,
     Till the incorruptible core of the wood remains lustrous.
     Oft with this cane I have crossed a ford, feeling my way,
     Often in my wandering, I have saved myself from calamity.
     This cane, however, leans aimlessly against a sunny wall,
     And its service has been ignored longer than I can count.

39. Priest as I am, I but honor the behests of the western sky.
(66) I hid myself at Mt. Kugami, and stopped counting the years.
     All my garments are threadbare like thinning mist or smoke.
     I wander around, supporting my weight upon my crooked cane.
     Removed to a distant valley, I recite poems to my own ears.
     Planting myself upon a stone, I watch silver clouds gather.
     Yet, my heart is heavy for this world's sake, and the fame
     Man seeks spinning through life, like dust before the wind.

40. The full length of a dark winter night is just its length,
(67) Long and slow-moving, as I once found it upon my cold bed.
There was no life in the candle, no heat in the fireplace.
My face on the pillow, I hearkened to the night-long rain.

41. As the thoughts of my boyhood return to me in this old age,
(69) I often picture myself reading a book alone in a huge hall.
The burning candle before me has been replaced many a time.
In those days I knew not the full length of a winter night.

42. Taken by illness, I lay upon my back, altogether helpless.
(71) Oft my spirit searched in a dream the sights once visited.
This morning, I rose, and dragged my feet to a river-bank.
I saw peach blossoms flowing ceaselessly after the stream.

43. My haggard face is so wasted that it obscures the mirror.
(72) My frosty hair is long enough to produce twisted tangles.
The lips fever-dry incessantly thirst for a moist relief.
The black skin wrapped in filth craves immediate washing.
Burning heat and icy chill dispute for power in my flesh,
And my pulse fails, having fallen in a mire of confusion.
Only woodcutters' talk reaches my ears through the woods,
To acquaint me of the half of February lost all too soon.

44. Imprisoned by the walls of my hermitage I lie upon my back.
(73) For a whole day, not a soul comes to pay me a kindly visit.
My begging bag hangs slack, with my bowl in its empty womb.
My walking stick has surrendered itself to the piling dust.
Dreams go their ways, revolving around the hills and moors.
My spirit returns to the city where it once found pleasure.
At the busy street corners, I have not the slightest doubt,
Many boys are expecting me to return as a matter of course.

45. For three months this spring, I lay sick in my lonely house.
(76) One day, a visitor wanted my brush work on a sheet of paper.
     I shut my eyes and remembered that this day the year before
     I had played at a village shrine till dusk took me unawares.

46. Since I shed my black hair and took vows as a holy priest,
(77) My feet have carried me for years through grass and winds.
     Till today they thrust at me everywhere a brush and paper,
     Telling me but to make, but to write poems for their sake.

47. What destiny has put together myself and this writing-brush?
(78) Having laid it down, I take it again at my friend's request.
     Failing to unriddle this mystery, I have none to comfort me
     But the infinite He who has tamed the sins and walks heaven.

48. In the depth of a quiet night I draw my ink slab towards me.
(80) My face aglow with wine, I drop my well-worn brush to paper.
     In my poems, I try to equal plum blossoms in sweet opulence.
     A dying stock, I shall not yield to budding shoots like you.

49. Mile after mile I tramped till I chanced on a farm house.
(81) The sun was about to drop its fiery ball behind a forest.
     Sparrows had gathered themselves around a bamboo thicket.
     They flew about in the closing dark all in a noisy flock.
     Presently a farmer came home from his work in the fields.
     He had hardly seen me before he greeted me as his friend.
     He told his wife to strain the cloudy wine to welcome me,
     And with his garden vegetables, he treated me to a feast.
     We sat down across a table, to drink each other's health.
     Our conversation that night was beyond the worldly level.
     We drank till we were both tipsy, and in our elated mood,
     Neither of us knew for sure right or wrong here on earth.

50. One day, in summer, when rice plants were coming into ear,
(83) I went out of my gate, swinging my belled cane to and fro.
I had not gone many a mile on my way when in a paddyfield
A farmer saw me, stopped me, forced me to stay for a chat.
A plain reed mat spread on the ground served for our seat,
And we ate from wide paulownia leaves used for our plates.
Under the gay sky, we passed our cordial cups a few times,
Till I was tipsy, and fell asleep, my skull on the ground.

51. True, all the seasons have moonlit nights,
(84) But here's the best night to see the moon.
The hills never so aloft, the streams never so clear,
In the infinite blue of autumn sky flies a disk of light.
Neither light nor gloom is graced with a life of its own.
The moon and the earth are one, and myself one with them.
The boundless sky above, and autumn chill on my skin,
I stroll about low hills, leaning upon my priceless cane.
Quiet night has held firm the flitting dust of the world.
The bright moon alone pours streams of rays all about me.
I mind it not if another like-minded is also admiring it,
Or if the moon deigns to look on others as well as on me.
Each year as autumn comes, the moon will shine as before,
And the world will watch it, will face it, till eternity.
Sermons at Mt. Ryōzen, lectures in the Vale of Sōkei,
Were teachings so precious, the audience needed the moon.
My meditation under the moon lasts till the ripest night.
The stream has hushed its cry, dew lies thick everywhere.
Who, among the moon-viewers tonight, will have the prize?
Who will reflect the purest moon in the lake of his mind?
Surely you all know of that riverside moon-viewing of long ago,
When Fugan alone, the rest lagging, ran beyond the flesh,
And of Yakkyō who, moon-inspired, cracked a laugh on a hilltop?
Their reputation rose high, when the feats were reported,
But over a thousand years intervene between now and then.
Men have watched for naught the vicissitudes of the moon.
I am, nonetheless, swayed in my thoughts by the ancients.
Tonight, I keep a bright vigil, my robes soaked in tears.

52. One bitterly blighted day, in the gray month of November,
(87) Snow descended on us, while we were benighted by a gloom.
In the beginning, the flakes looked hard like sandy salt.
Later, they were more like the downy flowers of a willow.
They fell upon bamboo twigs with rustles in their leaves.
They piled on pine branches, forming many strange shapes.
Not quite ready yet to open the books of ancient masters,
I found mounting in my dark self a desire to write poems.

53. It once grew in the heavenly country far away in the west.
(88) No one knows how many years since its coming to the world.
Its white petals are wrapped in a profusion of shiny dews.
Its rare-green leaves spread everywhere in the round lake.
Chaste is its scent wafted over the fence by a quiet wind.
Arrestingly calm, its whole poise as it rises above water.
The sun has already hid itself behind the hills before me
But I cannot move a step for the charm of the lotus plant.

54. Now I sing the glory of the bamboo trees around my house.
(89) Several thousands stand together, forming a placid shade.
Young shoots run wild, blocking the roads here and there.
Old branches stretch all the way, cutting across the sky.
Frosty winters have armed them with a spiritual strength.
Rising mists wrap them with the veil of profound mystery.
In their healthy beauty they even rank with pine and oak,
Although they do not vie in grandeur with peach and plum.
Their trunks are upright and their knots are far between.
Their hearts are void of stuffing and their roots sturdy.
Bamboo trees, I admire you for your honesty and strength.
Be my friends, and stand about my retreat until eternity.

55. Several miles beyond the city wall stands the house of Tō.
(90) I walk toward it, led by the woodcutter I chanced to meet.
On either side of the footpath rises a row of green pines.
Over the valley, the scent of a wild plum is wafted to me.
Each visit to this place yields me a fresh spiritual gain.

Where else can I lay aside my cane and stand at full ease?
In the ancient pond swarm fishes big enough to be dragons.
Quiet holds the enclosing woods, and the day moves slowly.
Within the house itself, not a hoard of worldly treasures,
But a jumble of books in verse and prose spread on a desk.
Flushed with inspiration, I loosen myself and my garments.
Gleaning some words from old masters, I make my own poems.
When the twilight comes, I stroll out to the east veranda.
A spring bird, an earlier visitor, greets me on its wings.

56. Soon as springtime warmth tempers the month of February,
(92) Plums and peaches begin to spread their varied blossoms.
Some are so high, they rise over the tops of the houses.
Others, lower than the garden fence, creep on the earth.
Brighter than the sun, they all glow tenderly colourful.
Their scent flies higher than eventide mists and clouds.
Princes arrive in their coaches to banquet beneath them.
Ladies walk, hand in hand, in the garden to admire them.
There is no telling, however, when a mad storm will hit.
They will then be swept along like snow to bury the city.

57. High on a rocky hill, at the temple named Great Sorrow,
(95) I hold my chin in my hands, and watch far clouds glide.
Tall pines about me rise straight up to the hollow sky.
The winds, old as the world itself, send me chaste air.
Far below me, there rises a spring named Dragon's Well.
Its water is so pure, the pebbled floor shows flawless.
Let me call in my loudest voice to each wayfarer I see,
Come, and see yourself mirrored in this spotless glass.

58. Here are the ruins of the cottage where I once hid myself.
(99) Revisited now in stark solitude, my cane alone at my side.
The fences have tumbled over the walks of foxes and hares.
The well has dried up, nearly covered over by rank bamboo.
Cobwebs hang slack at the window, where I once had a desk.
The floor I sat upon for long meditation has sunk in dust.

The garden steps have fallen under the bushy autumn grass.
Crickets alone raise their cries as if in defiance of man.
Loth to leave this place, I maunder around for many hours,
Till, appalled at the twilight, I watch the declining sun.

59. Not a stray bird flies over the range of remote hills.
(101) In the secluded garden, leaves fall one after another.
In the autumn wind that breathes cheerless desolation
A man is standing by himself, wrapped in a black gown.

60. This morning, the shrine gate has a pile of silver snow.
(102) All the trees on the holy ground shine, as with flowers.
Who may it be, I keep thinking, the boy out in the cold,
Throwing snowballs, as if the world existed all for him.

61. The big river is at a flood level, the spring nearly over.
(105) The downy flowers of willow trees fall on my gown sleeves.
Far beyond in the gathering mist, a fishing boat whistles.
Who will ease me of this infinite melancholy in my breast?

62. Too foggy to earn my own livelihood ever since I was born,
(110) For good or evil, I have just let events take their shape.
Within my begging sack, I have but three handfuls of rice.
By my fireplace, a bundle of dry branches to keep me warm.
I pursue not the subtle difference between true and false.
I aspire not to gain the dust of worldly fame and fortune.
On a damp night, secure under the roof of my grassy house,
I stretch out both my legs, my conscience perfectly clear.

A reply to a friend
63.
(111) Such is my bigoted stupidity, I cannot live with any man.
Befriended by trees and herbs, I pass my declining years.
Too idle to learn the difference between right and wrong,

I laugh at my old self, not caring what others might say.
Lifting my bony shanks, I cross a running stream at ease.
A sack in my hand, I walk about, blest by spring weather.
Living in this way, I lack not my life's bare sustenance.
Never once have I harboured wry hatred against the world.

64. Tatters, nothing but tatters, are the garments on my back,
(116) And what else but tatters is left of my life, at this age?
Seated on a wayside stone, I eat food given me in charity;
I have long surrendered my house to the encroaching weeds.
On a moonlit night, I sit up singing poems to my own ears.
Led astray by the flowers, I roam away till I lose myself.
Ever since I left the temple where I was once an inquirer,
By my own sheer folly, I have sunk to this wretched state.

65. In my youth, I threw aside my writing brush and ink slab,
(117) And pined in my heart for the life of the ancient saints.
Then, nothing but a flask and a bowl in my begging hands,
I wandered far and wide, no one knows for how many years.
Having at last come home, in the shade of a cragged hill,
At a weedy cottage I found the restful life of a recluse.
I have since lived alone, turning to songbirds for music,
And for my friends I have white clouds rising in the sky.
Beneath a massive rock, a spring swells in a fair stream,
Whose clear water washes the dust from my black garments.
Near the ridges, tall pines and oaks rise towards heaven;
Their branches and leaves give me warmth in cold weather.
With nothing to worry me, not a care to disturb my peace,
I live from day to day till the day dawns no more for me.

66. A warm easterly wind has brought with it a timely rain.
(118) It pours softly on the thatched roof in the deep night.
The lord of the house dozes, his head on a high pillow.
Asleep or awake, he knows not the tricks of this world.
The dawn comes, bathing the green hills in fresh light.
The spring birds twitter in every branch of the forest.

Rising from my sleep, I walk cheerfully out at my gate
And roam about, following the wind rather than my will.
Streams run through the field to soak a far-off hamlet.
Blossoms blaze upon the slopes of the rare-green hills.
Whoever he is, I see an aged man with a cow behind him,
And a youth, wherever his home, with a hoe on his back.
Everything on earth is busy at its work, never staying,
And for all I know, every man has a duty in his charge.
Who am I, the lord of an empty house, to stand useless,
Chained by the bond of attachment to my native village.

67.   Void of fleshly desire, I find satisfaction in all things.
(121) Nothing is big enough to cure man's desire, once awakened.
Wild vegetables are quite sufficient to gratify my hunger.
The gown I have on my flesh keeps me wrapped against cold.
I range all by myself, stags and harts keeping me company.
I sing loudly to myself, children answering me in harmony.
By a mossy rock, I have a clear spring to wash my ears in.
Upon the ridges, tall pines to comfort me in my sore need.

68.   I think of the past, to realize it is gone beyond recall.
(123) I try to think of the present, but it never stays for me.
Time glides slowly away, leaving not a trace in its wake.
Who can be wise or foolish in this constant flux of time?
I live day to day, quietly accepting my share of destiny.
I sustain my life, and wait till I am released from time.
After long wandering abroad, I came here to this cottage,
Now twenty years ago, as I look back upon the years gone.

69.   As soon as peaceful harmony makes itself known in the sky,
(129) I flick my cane and leave my gate, to enjoy a spring walk.
Streams run with a tiny murmur on the floor of the valley,
And the forests echo with the soft music of singing birds.
If I meet a priest on my way, I walk with him for a while.
If a friend, I follow him home for a restful conversation.
Truly, this life of mine, with what can I best compare it
But that boat, released of its mooring, drifting offshore?

70. Now that August has arrived, a cool breeze begins to blow.
(130) Water-fowl fly southward in their journey across the seas.
I, too, leave my house to wander away, a flask in my hand.
Down the green hill road I make haste, possessed with joy.
If I meet a priest by chance, I leave my road to join him.
If a wanderer like myself, I walk by his side for company.
Truly, this life of mine, with what can I best compare it
But those weeds, afloat on the water, blown by the breeze?

71. No longings have I in my heart to seek life's gay flowers.
(132) With hills and streams for my friends, I live free as air.
I let the clouds swallow my shadow, as I walk on the road.
Birds often fly over my head, as I sit resting on a stone.
My straw sandals heavy with snow, I visit frozen villages.
A cane in my hand, I range the spring fields on fair days.
Deep enough have I probed into the truth of our existence
To know the glory of spring flowers is but a form of dust.

72. Far and wide I roamed, but nowhere could I ease my heart.
(134) I have at last come home to this retreat in a sordid row.
During the day, I must bear the lies of world-crazed men,
And at night, the rotten talk of my garrulous neighbours.
My hollow room has its dole of "the white rays" at times,
But my hearthstones stand unheated for many days running.
Even so, let it be; no word of protest will move my lips.
I accept all, for all is given me as my share of destiny.

73. The red coral has its home on the floor of the south sea;
(136) The purple lawn grows lush on the slopes of arctic hills.
Everything alive on earth has its home as its birthright,
Defined, not as it grows, but at the time of its genesis.
Once in my green years, I chanced to forsake my homeland,
And trusting myself to a cane, I roamed a thousand miles.
Many a time on the doors of aged teachers I gave a knock,
And under their guidance, suffered autumns of discipline.
My purpose was to build a broad thoroughfare of my faith.

I never grudged to use my flesh, froth-weak as I knew it.
Alas, the years have slid away faster than I could dream!
Now I am at a loss what to say about myself, so timeworn.
Having returned to where I belong, to a house by a cliff,
I gather early and late wild bracken sprouts for my fare.

74. October has brought with it wintry blasts and icy chill.
(139) I rose with the sun, and down the hill I went by myself.
The trees around me were all rid of their summer leaves.
The streams were winter-dry and voiceless on their beds.
I turned my head, and cast a far glance at a south hill,
Where I found pines and oaks firm in their proud vigour.
In this season when all things droop, fall, and scatter,
Pines and oaks alone have the strength to defy the cold.
What about me, I asked myself, but the answer failed me.
Pines and oaks before my eyes, I sang their loud praise.

75. Many a time in my youth, I sat down for long meditation,
(140) Hoping to master by practice the art of quiet breathing,
And in this study I spent many years of frost and stars,
Till I was quite oblivious of my meals and my own sleep.
What virtue I now have in me to foster my heart's peace,
I owe it to the hard discipline I underwent in my youth.
Alas, what am I to speak thus, lacking that artless art
Wherein all is learned but once, all forever to be mine?

76. With the sun, everything on earth falls into deep repose.
(141) I, too, return home, and close my cottage door behind me.
The cries of crickets are already scarce and far between.
The trees and grass have lost their proud summer colours.
The long night often requires a new filling of my censer.
Chill on my skin forces upon me a pile of thick garments.
Let us use our diligence while we may, my gentle friends,
Time flies like an arrow and lingers not a moment for us.

77. *A debate in a dream*
(143) On my begging round, I happened to enter a thriving city.
An old man with a brow of deep wisdom met me in the road.
He stopped me with the question, Why is it, Reverend Sir,
You live far away on a hilltop, below those white clouds?
I, in return, inquired of him, Why is it, my Good Master,
You have so long spent your life in the roar of the city?
Both tried to answer, and searched in vain for apt words,
But my dream was broken at the tolling of a morning bell.

78. Envy not for once, my noble friend, my careless freedom.
(144) Satisfaction can be got wherever there is heart's peace.
Who in a thousand knows that seldom in these blue hills
Are tigers and wolves found to range in the secret dark?

79. Whoever reads my poetry, and calls it poetry by its name,
(145) I know he is in grave error, for my poetry is not poetry.
After you have learned my poetry is unworthy of its name
I will sit down to discuss with you the secret of my art.

80. Since I left the holy temple wherein my teacher presided,
(149) Free in my simple ignorance, I have spent many idle days.
I have kept beside me a single cane to support my weight.
My garments have melted away like loose threads of smoke.
Facing a blank window, I hearken to the rain of midnight.
I bounce balls in a street, thriving in springtime glory.
Should anyone kindly question me by the wayside who I am,
I would but present myself as an idle man in an idle age.

81. Choked by the smell of herbs, a spring day falls to dark.
(150) Dotted with peach blossoms, a river goes its endless way.
I am by nature unmindful of the sly wisdom of this world.
Bewitched by the charm of spring, I cannot rest my heart.

82. Aboard the boats from far-off provinces, sailors are busy.
(153) Some sing their native songs, others play gay instruments.
     I was away in the calm of a mountain temple but yesterday,
     A butterfly, revelling like the sailors in a vernal dream.

83.   *An answer to the priest Tenge's poem on the New Year*
(155) Alas, man lingers here but as a horse runs through a gate.
     Year after year, he piles up the debts he intended to pay.
     Tomorrow, another year will come, if I can trust my sense.
     I am already a man of grizzled hair and beard, time-taken.
     Before me, riverside willows are swinging their soft arms,
     But plums are not yet graced with fragrance upon the hill.
     I lack the wings to fly a million miles against the storm.
     Ungifted, I echo the phoenix on yonder hill in my singing.

84. It was a whim of destiny that brought me under my teacher.
(156) After a while, I left his temple to fall into my own ways.
     Free from hunger, freed from sickness, I now live content,
     Contemporary of ancient sages and old leaders of my faith.

85. I left my family, my own home, to seek wisdom far abroad.
(158) Just a gown and a bowl with me, I wandered many a spring.
     Today, I have returned, to visit friends of my past days.
     Alas, many of them sleep under mossy stones but as names.

86. After a few years of wandering about in far-off provinces,
(160) Today, I have returned home to the sacred shrine of Otogo.
     Know me, my friends, to be safe from the ills of the road,
     By the lights, bright as before in the sockets of my eyes.

87. In my green years, I left my father and ran to a stranger.
(163) I have laboured since to draw a tiger, painting but a cat.
     Should anyone inquire of me now what I think about myself,
     I would answer, I am just as I was in youth, Eizō by name.

88.   As a boy, I studied the arts, failing to become a scholar.
(165) In youth, I studied zen, failing to obey my master's lamp.
      I now live in a grassy cottage, merged in a Shinto shrine,
      Not unlike a shrine-keeper, or unlike a prophet of Buddha.

89.   This busy world transforms itself like wind-driven clouds.
(167) Some fifty years of my life seem to me one unbroken dream.
      Late at night, as quiet showers fall on my grassy cottage,
      I embrace my holy gown, and lean against my hollow window.

90.   For sixty years and more I have been but an ailing priest.
(169) My cottage is beside a shrine, away from the smoking town.
      Late at night, rains flood down, rooting up massive rocks.
      Before my dark window the candlelight falters in the wind.

91.   I am more than seventy, as I look back upon my years gone.
(171) I have known the rights and wrongs of men, till I am sick.
      On this night of deep snow, hardly a trace of man in view,
      A rod of incense gives off a trail of smoke by the window.

92.   Good manners and sweet habits have faded, year after year.
(172) Both court and country have sunk down, one age to another.
      Men's hearts have grown stiff and stony, as time descends.
      The First Teacher's steps have dimmed, after hard wearing.
      Leaders of numerous sects cry out beliefs of their making.
      Their disciples shout even louder to promote their causes.
      Leaders and disciples alike stick together on their guard.
      On peril of their lives, they do not yield to their enemy.
      If, in religion, sects rule absolute, each in its dignity,
      Who, amid the ancient saints, could not have taken a lead?
      And if each man, in his own power, wishes to found a sect,
      Alas, I know not where I might find a proper place for me.
      Leaders of different sects, stay your quarrelling a while,
      And bend your slow ears to what I have to say on my faith.

My faith has trickled down far away from its chief source;
Who preached at Mt. Ryōzen is whom I must first recommend.
He has climbed, beyond our reach, to the zenith of heaven.
No one alive has wisdom enough to know his right or wrong.
About five hundred years after he sank into eternal gloom,
Learned men began to interpret his teachings in many ways,
Until a great man was born unto this world, a guide to us,
Who sorted out problems and wove a subtle web of thinking.
He, moreover, acted out what he thought right in his view,
So again, no one can aspire to discuss his right or wrong.
By and by, my faith found its way into an eastern country,
Where its sole foundation was built at the temple, Hakuba.
Into this country came, through hardships, a wise teacher,
And placed under his leadership sects then in mortal feud.
It was during the well-governed reign of the T'ang Dynasty,
When the flowers of wisdom budded and bloomed all at once.
People listened to him and followed him with high respect.
He led the sects in full accord, like a lion in the woods.
Signs of disintegration were rank shortly after his death,
But the sad split between north and south came much later.
It was but in the last troublous days of the Sung Dynasty,
When the white wall of Zen tumbled to the pressure of men.
Then the so-called five schools began to lift their heads,
And they together opposed the proud eight sects for power.
The result was naught but confusion followed by confusion.
Alas, no one is alive now who can put it right by his wit.
My faith took root in my native land at the temple, Eihei,
Planted there by a man who rose by himself above the rest.
This man bore his master's seal far away from Mt. Taihaku,
And founded his solid fame in my country, loud as thunder.
What he chose to teach in his books caused wonder and awe.
Even fierce elephants and dragons would have been quelled.
Many have walked along the highway of faith marked by him,
And arrived in the regions of pure light, lit by his fire.
His books are free from needless quibbles and repetitions,
And contain all we ever need to study about our salvation.
Alas, since the teacher left my country, this divine land,
I know not how many ages have slipped in quick succession;

During which time, weeds rose to oppress the house of Zen,
And herbs of fragrance have all drooped, unable to resist.
Who, amid the holies now, can move sun-warm lips like his,
When the cries of self-sacred divines daily tire the town?
I cannot arrest the surge of sorrow in my heart, for I am
A weak man come to the world to face its worst in history.
When the whole frame threatens to tumble down through rot,
How can I, a single man, carry its weight on my shoulders?
One quiet night, deprived of sleep, my eyes under a spell,
I rolled over many times in my bed, and wrote these lines.

93. Since I shed my black hair, and became a wandering priest,
(173) I have depended on charity for the sustenance of my flesh.
Fully aware of what I am, how beggarly I must go each day,
I have not the least pride in me to slacken self-reproach.
How is it, then, the divines of the world, as I hear them,
Cry aloud to advance their empty words by day or by night?
But to serve their mouths and stomachs, so it seems to me,
They have lost themselves, and sent their hearts far away.
When I see ordinary men of the world fallen in mortal sin,
I can sympathize with them and forgive them for ignorance.
But you who have vowed to uphold the holy way of a priest,
How can you suffer yourselves to be so smeared with filth?
You are rid of your hair, to rend your attachment to life.
You wear a black robe, to show all colours are but shades.
You have abandoned all your human obligations, to be free,
At an equal distance away from the worldly right or wrong.
When I go on my begging round each morning before sunrise,
I see men and women busy doing their duties in the fields.
If they do not spin, how can they cover their naked limbs?
If they do not till, how will they gratify their stomachs?
The self-appointed disciples of Buddha alone live useless,
Wholly unemployed in works, wholly undisciplined in faith.
They devour the good will of their unsuspecting adherents.
Neglectful of the deeds of their limbs, mouths and hearts.
They put their heads together, to revel in grandiloquence.
Taken by this old vice, they know not either dawn or dusk.
They present their respectful brows for the world to view,

But trapping innocent old women is all that they care for.
If successful, they think themselves the cleverest of men.
Ah, when will they stop dreaming and come to their senses?
Much better it were to be thrown into the paths of tigers
Than to find yourself lost in the labyrinth of false fame.
If a grain of proud desire forces its way into your heart,
With all the water of the sea, you cannot purge its stain.
Since your leave-taking, what do you consider your father
Has been doing for your sake, early and late, at his home?
With fumes of incense on the altar, he prays to every god
For your continuous devotion to your religious discipline.
If you be really such as you are, or such as you now seem,
I cannot but wish you had not made your vow to begin with.
We all stay in this life but as a wayfarer does at an inn.
Men's lives expire as fast as morning dews before the sun.
Opportunities are much sooner lost than got in all things.
In religion, you come on a true teacher but once or twice.
Therefore, do not break off till you shine in true lustre,
Nor stand idle, waiting for others to call on you to wake.
I have thrust upon you these numerous words of admonition,
Not because I take delight in giving unsolicited counsels,
But in the honest hope that you will so search your heart,
That you may correct your manners, not tomorrow but today.
Let us use our best diligence, friends who will follow me,
Lest we should, some day, repent of our failures in youth.

94. As I mark the priests who have left their teachers to roam,
(174) Alas, I cannot but pity them, for they are green, each one.
They seem to think, unless known at the three head temples,
They are absolutely disgraced as members of the holy order.
This is why they have rashly given their teachers the slip
And roam from one place to another, relying on their canes,
To spend one summer at one temple they happened to stay at,
And to pass at another temple the three months of a winter.
To imitate the styles of sundry teachers they have visited
Is all the business they bear in mind in their daily talks.
Throw at them one searching word, when they light upon you.
You will know them, as before, green enough to excite pity.

95. Look at the preacher, interpreting passages of holy sutras.
(175) Such is his fluency, a river runs not so fast as his words.
On the Five Mystical Stages and the Eight Blissful Methods
He can comment so well, no one can exceed him in eloquence.
He recognizes himself as a learned man, wise in everything,
And the world raises no objection to this self-borne title.
Nonetheless, search him for the secret mystery of our life.
Not a word of just reply will leak out of his silent mouth.

96. Once upon a time, at the holy temple of Shakutai Kannon In,
(178) A group of ten blessed hearts lived united in full harmony.
They put their hands together, to perform their daily work.
They joined in holy talks, all equal in honour and respect.
They sat in their hall for ninety days of quiet meditation.
However employed, they raced with time, free from idleness.
Now everyone will agree, never again a group of holy sages
Such as this one will make its appearance in years to come.

97. Whence has this life of mine arrived at its present abode,
(179) And after its departure, whereto is it destined to vanish?
Seated below the sagebrush window of my cottage by myself,
I meditated on these questions, mute in the dead of night.
I searched my heart many times, but the answers failed me.
Neither the wherefrom, nor the whereto, of my life I know.
Equally unknown to me is my life's existence here and now,
For all the world is in a nimble flux, and void therefore.
I am suspended mid-air in the vacuity but for a twinkling.
How am I supposed to know the subtlety of right and wrong?
I must perforce receive what descends on me as my destiny,
And live accordingly, while I may, with careless serenity.

98. Ancient sages left their works behind, not to let us know
(181) About themselves, but to help us understand our own stamp.
Had we wisdom deep enough to know ourselves single-handed,
No benefits would result from the works of ancient saints.

A wise man learns the mystery of his existence in a flash
And climbs in a leap beyond the world of hollow phenomena,
Whereas a foolish man holds wilfully to facts and details,
To drown himself in subtle differences of words and lines,
And being envious of others in their supreme achievements,
He wastes his mind night and day in his efforts to exceed.
Truth, if you cleave to it as truth, turns into falsehood.
Falsehood, when you see it as such, becomes at once truth.
Truth and falsehood are the mated edges of a double sword.
None alive can separate with certainty one from the other.
Alas, too many men drift with the skiff to fathom the sea.
From time immemorial they are causes of endless deception.

99.   Sweet saintliness is to be sought as a work of your heart.
(185) The rightful path lies not amid things of constant change.
      This plainest truth must be implanted time and time again,
      Lest you should fall a witless victim to deceiving voices.
      If you turn your shafts northward, hoping to travel south,
      Alas, how can you ever arrive at your desired destination?

100. In its innocence, the heart is like water pure and bright.
(186) Boundless it presents itself to the sight of its beholder.
      Should a proud desire rise, however, to disturb its peace,
      Millions of wicked thoughts and pictures will bog it down.
      If you take these fancies to be real enough to engage you,
      You will be led farther and farther away from tranquility.
      How sore it is to see a man crazed about earthly thoughts,
      A heart bound closely by the cords of the ten temptations.

101. To hear the words of truth, you must wash your ears clean.
(196) You will not, otherwise, stand true to what you will hear.
      You will ask what it is I mean by washing your ears clean.
      It means to rid yourself of all you have heard beforehand.
      If only one word of your previous learning remains within,
      You will fail to embrace the words, when they come to you.

Resembling what you know, a plain lie may seem acceptable,
And a simple truth, strange to your ears, may sound false.
How often, alas, we have our judgments made in our hearts,
When truth lies outside, in a place beyond our conception.
Let us not commit such folly as to steep a stone in water,
To hide it for a moment, knowing it will show in due time.

102. Beauty is still accompanied in this world by vile ugliness.
(198) Truth cannot be, unless mated to its counterpart falsehood.
Wisdom and folly come from the same source, though unknown.
Blind delusion and wakeful enlightenment walk side by side.
Since time immemorial, it has always been as I have stated,
And you must have marked it for yourself long before I did.
To cast away one thing as false, taking up another as true,
Is little more than to indulge in the dream of a twinkling.
Once vowed to the profound mystery shrouded in these words,
Who will commit himself to ever-changing rights and wrongs?

103. Words come sweeping out of your mouth, when your lips move.
(202) Your arms are slow to act, be you anxious to use them well.
You often try to cover up with your ready-to-flow speeches
What your lazy arms have not quite succeeded in performing.
The harder you try to polish, the more you spoil your work.
The more words you pour out, the greater evils you provoke.
Let us not commit such folly as to flood the fire with oil,
To cool it down for a moment, knowing it will soon explode.

104. Do not drive after this or that thing in your mad pursuit.
(204) Lock up your lips in deep reticence to do your daily work.
Never fill your mouth till hunger revolts in your stomach,
Nor rattle your teeth until you are fully awake and aware.
Ever since I learned what I know about the life of Hakuyū,
I have some means at least to sustain myself in the world.
Master your breath, so you may be tense with inner spirit.
No ills, then, can break into your heart from the outside.

105.   As I cast my eyes about me, to learn how men live on earth,
(210) I see them all busy trying to satisfy their hungry desires,
       And lagging far behind what they strive so hard to possess,
       They fret, mourn, and torture themselves into deep despair.
       Be they ever so lucky as to seize the prize in their palms,
       How long, let me ask them, could they hold it as their own?
       For every blissful pleasure they seek to win in this world,
       Ten times they must rack themselves with the pangs of hell.
       Ah, how can they find peace by trading anguish for anguish,
       To stay forever caught in the tangles which bind them fast?
       To use a simile, they are like the apes on a moonlit night
       That in their mad appetite to grab the silver disk of moon,
       Shedding its bright beams, halfway across a running stream,
       Leap one after another into the fathomless whirlpool below.
       Alas, I cannot but take pity on the proud men of the world,
       For they are doomed to an endless struggle, robbed of rest.
       Tears run down my face, in spite of myself, as I sit alone,
       And muse on man's wretched state over and over in the dark.

106.   Such is the power of mutability that all our lives perish,
(211) This minute and this minute, faster than any can foretell.
       A youth's rosy cheeks wither, no matter how we prize them.
       A man's bushy hairs droop till they are thin like strings.
       Years weigh on your backs till your bone bends like a bow.
       The skin on your weary face wrinkles like the ruffled sea.
       A noise like that of a cicada attacks your ears all night.
       Flowers flitter in your eyes all day, dazzling your sense.
       When you rise or sit, you must vent out a long windy sigh,
       And when you walk, you must support your weight on a cane.
       You chase in your dreams the memories of your happy youth,
       And count in despair the miseries of your over-ripe years.
       How else can I describe the wretched state of an aged man,
       But to compare it with a broken bough flung away in frost?
       Yet we all must come to this state, sooner than we expect,
       For time never spares us, once we are born in frail flesh.
       Time creeps on, minute by minute, without a moment's stay,
       And how long can we retain our youthful days against time?

The elements that constitute our flesh languish every day,
And, nightly, sick dullness overspreads our mind and body.
One morning you will find yourself far too weak to get up.
Then for many days following, you must lie upon your back.
The lips that you once used to whip others with eloquence,
What use do they have now, when you must sleep in silence?
Once your breath fails and leaves your body in sad stupor,
All the instruments of your perception lose their virtues.
Your friends and relatives will watch your face and mourn.
Your own family will lament, passing their hands over you.
However desperately they may call, you cannot answer them.
However loudly they may cry, you can never recognize them.
For you are already well on your way to timeless darkness.
Alas, you must make this solitary journey all by yourself.

107. How short, and how deplorable, is man's life on the earth!
(213) A hundred years' joy once past is just a springtime dream.
Soon as our breath fails, we are already out of the world.
We are men, as long as the four elements dwell in harmony.
What is all this, then, I hear about men fighting proudly
For fame and gains, like heroes, in defiance of other men?
Come, I pray you to cast your eye through the windy gloom
Over the sagebrush moors, dotted with unearthed skeletons.

108. I walked out of my house, and came to a shadowy hill road.
(215) Rows of ancient gravestones stood about me on either side.
Among the pines and oaks, older far than a thousand years,
The wind blew, from dawn till dusk, with a sorrowful wail.
The writings on the stones had dimmed so through exposure,
Even sons and daughters could not read the parents' names.
When I saw it, hot tears rose in me, and choked my breath.
I walked off on my cane, only to retrace my steps halfway.

109. None have the skill to measure the broad highway of faith.
(217) It leads on and on, and no one knows whereunto it will go.
Take a stage for an end, and you can not reach even there.

Dream to awake from a dream, and you must stay in reverie.
What if you know how to preach upon existence and vacuity?
How can you hold the middle way, if you see where it lies?
Wordless is the mystery of this stage where I find myself;
Directly that mystery reaches my idle teeth, it breaks up.

110. The great highroad of faith is like a brimless receptacle.
(218) It stands infinite, and none have the skill to measure it.
The thoughts and feelings of average men spend themselves,
And their rights and wrongs end in more rights and wrongs.
In the bibble-babble, who knows there is a mysterious way?
I walk along it, all by myself, my lips locked in silence.
Should I see another road, easier than the one of Nirvana,
I know how foul it would present itself to cloudless eyes.

111. The way of truth presents a view, much superior to others,
(220) But men of this world stand outside, forever in ignorance.
They avail themselves of causes and reasons utterly alien,
To explain the mystery which falls back farther from them.
The Great Man of the Plum Hill espied truth in a sentence,
And Enō succeeded his master, though called Beastly Blind.
Men of high spirit, I urge you to keep your courage stout.
Vowed to truth, do not frisk east and west like a feather.

112. The wind has dropped to a dead calm, but the flowers fall.
(223) The birds are singing merrily, but silence rules the hill.
This is the miracle, wrought by the virtue of wise Kannon.
Inscrutable!

113. Stay your mad quest for the rich jewels of Konkō and Gōho,
(225) For I have a spotless jewel within the limits of my heart.
Beyond the sun and the moon, it shines to the darkest end.
Such is its radiance that it pierces and blinds every eye.
Without it, I must settle in the deep sea of self-torture.
Now, my friends, I pray you, accept this jewel as my gift.
Alas, no one cares enough about it to bend his ears to me.

114.   Shut within the confines of this world, there lives a man,
(230) Permanently above the noisy reproach of fault-finding men.
       Whoever may crave an interview, he will not show his face.
       Only through a servant, he conveys his message to a guest.
       This man can raise a mountain by weaving filaments of air.
       He can also create surging waves by kneading still stones.
       From time to time, he walks by himself to a populous city,
       And stretching his hands at every house, he begs for alms.

115.   False delusion and true enlightenment sustain each other.
(231) Evident causes and secret reasons so merge, they are one.
       From morning to dusk, I read in silence my wordless text
       And, until dawn, I give myself to thoughtless meditation.
       Spring warblers whistle to me from wind-inspired willows.
       Dogs bark at me, as in alarm, far from a moonlit village.
       No laws can define the great surge of emotion filling me.
       How can I bequeath to posterity the heart so overwhelmed?

116.   You point with your finger to denote the moon in the sky,
(232) But the finger is blind unless the moon is shining there.
       What relation do you see between the moon and the finger?
       Are they two separate objects, or one and the same thing?
       This metaphorical question is asked as a handy expedient
       To inspire the beginners wrapped in the fog of ignorance.
       One who has learned to look into mystery beyond metaphor
       Knows that neither the moon nor the finger exists at all.

117.   Flowers have no close designs to lure butterflies to stay,
(233) Nor butterflies any ambition to take advantage of flowers,
       But butterflies do not dally far behind when flowers blow,
       And flowers bloom all at once as soon as butterflies come.
       I am a mere stranger to others about me, if not to myself.
       Conversely, they are strangers to me as much as I to them.
       Yet by a set of secret laws they and I are firmly chained.

118.   I hold in my hand a cane made of the horns of a wild hare.
(234) I enclose my flesh in a garment woven of filaments of air.
       I wear on my feet sandals fashioned of fine tortoise wool,
       And I sing poems in my silent voice, so everyone can hear.

119.   I went to rest in a wild moor, my skull on a grass-pillow,
(235) Still disturbed as I was by the rank cries of stray birds.
       Then the difference between the kings and the common herd
       Seemed just as absurd as the dream I saw during the night.

120.   Friends to help you, and teachers to lead you,
(237) You must try to maintain more than any riches.
       Wealth or poverty is as short-lived as an overnight dream.
       Loving words alone will breathe out perfume for a century.

121.   Book after book you can expound to advance your knowledge.
(238) Far better it is, though, to hold fast to a word of truth.
       What is it I mean by the word of truth, some might ask me.
       It means to come to terms with your heart as it really is.

122.   I sat alone, one dark spring night, already past midnight.
(244) Rain, mixed with some snow, poured onto the garden bamboo.
       I found no means to console myself in that solitary gloom.
       I reached for the holy book, written at the temple, Eihei.
       I lit my candle, and perfumed the air, before I opened it.
       I saw in every word and phrase a precious jewel contained.
       Now years ago, when I dwelled in Tamashima as a young man,
       My former teacher at the temple, Entsū,
       Read me the elements of this same book.
       Already, I had in my heart deepest respect for the author.
       I borrowed the book, and practised what I learned from it.
       Then it dawned on me that my former work had been a waste,
       So I obtained my teacher's leave, and roamed far and wide.
       Whatever has brought together this sacred book and myself,

I find, wherever I range, its teachings irresistibly true.
Teacher after teacher have I sought in my past wanderings.
Alas, no one gave me a lash, such as I felt from the book.
Laws and doctrines have I had many opportunities to study;
None convinced me so well as this book on my return to it.
We live in the age of mad confusion, steeped in ignorance.
We can hardly separate priceless jewels from false stones.
For five hundred years, this book has lain in sleepy dust,
Because none of us had eyes clear enough to see its value.
For whom, do you think, the author has put down his ideas?
Never take me for a cynic, applauding him at your expense.
That spring night, I sat and wept, with a light before me,
Till the book on my lap was thoroughly soaked in my tears.
The following day, I had a call from an old man next door.
As soon as he saw the book, he asked me why it was so wet.
I groped for an answer, for I sincerely hoped to tell him,
But for once my speech failed me, for I had my heart full.
After a short period of bowed silence, I found this reply.
A leak through the roof flooded my books during the night.

123.   *In honour of the skulls I drew on the scroll*
(245)
Whatever is born of a cause dies when that cause perishes.
Cause is tied to cause just as in a chain.
But what about the primary cause, could it rise causeless?
I searched all my heart, but I was at a loss as to the answer.
I took this sad tale to a woman in a house in the east.
She was more than displeased with my tale.
Next to a man in a hut in the west;
He gave me a puzzled frown, and turned away from me.
I wrote the tale on a rice-cake, and threw it to a dog.
Alas, the dog rejected it, the tale on it.
I realized then the ominous nature of my perplexing words,
And so, rolling up life and death together into a globule,
I gave it to the skulls lying on the moor.
Now the skulls uprose all at once in joyful ecstasy.
They sang lustily, they all danced for me.
The songs joined the three phases of time.

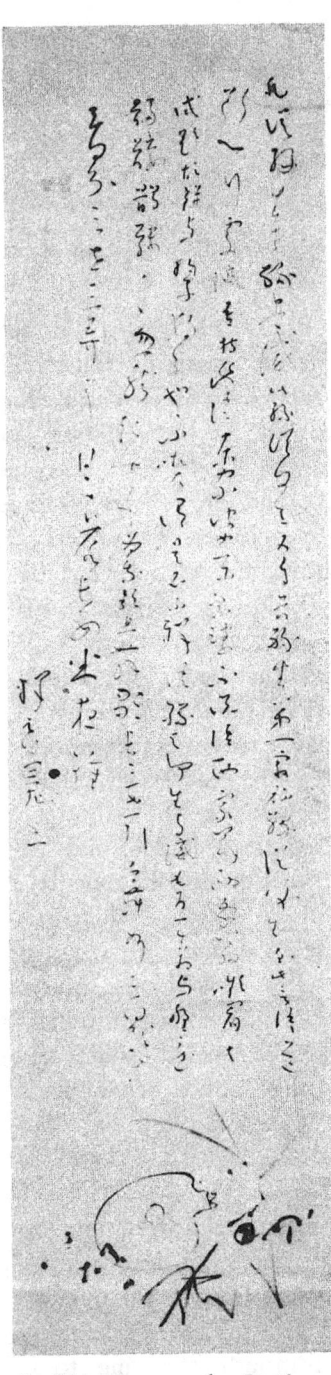

6. Chinese poem by Ryōkan
(No. 123)

The dance united the three stages of life.
Three phases and three stages they enacted three times,
Till the moon faded, as midnight was tolled from Chōan.

124.   *Shortly after an earthquake*
(248) Every day, day after day, yet at the return of another day,
Piercing cold rent my wrinkled skin, high noon or midnight.
The sky was wrapped in pitch-black clouds that hid the sun.
Whirlwinds swept the ground, rolling snow in their tongues.
Then, the quake struck the sea, sent limp fishes to heaven,
Blasted the earth, and drove men wailing from their houses.
As I glance back over the forty years preceding the ravage,
I must admit the world was on the decline, fast as a horse.
Accustomed to the luxury of peace, men's hearts became lax.
They conspired in banded factions and staged ghastly feuds.
Obligations were thrust out of the mind.
Truthful loyalty none cared to remember.
For profits, they battled to the finish.
They mocked the truths preached to them.
Too proud of themselves, they thought it business to cheat.
Pile on pile, they heaped shame, and knew not where to end.
The world was so full of this beastly kind, madly plotting,
I knew not whom to trust, to abate my heartfelt melancholy.
In all things, decay comes invisibly until the final wreck.
The quake was but a natural outcome, perhaps come too late.
Long before, the stars had veered away, though few knew it.
The seasons had been out of order, longer than any divined.
When you learn this, strike deeply into your own dark self,
And never, aping women and children, blame the world and heaven.

125. A young man, I knew, held the sunniest spot in the nation.
(249) Court and country alike paid decorous respect to his name.
People swarmed to his house, making a noise like a market.
His many rooms were full, for he had a houseful of guests.
One word from his mouth gave wings to pleading suppliants.
A swing of his arm moved a city from one place to another.

It is scarcely twenty years ago when I saw this young man.
Yet today the world behaves towards him colder than frost.

126. Many men I know in the world who crave this thing or that.
(253) They are like blind silkworms bound fast in their cocoons.
All for their incurable desires for this-worldly hoarding,
They have lost freedom, and worry their hearts and bodies.
Year after year, their native goodness loses its strength.
They become more rooted in their folly, as years multiply.
One morning, they strike out on their journey to eternity.
They must travel by themselves, not a penny to serve them.
What they have amassed, they leave for strangers to enjoy,
And their names shall be forgotten as soon as they depart.
Can anyone commit a greater folly than these helpless men?
Alas, they provoke infinite pity, deep in my heart's core.

127. As I look around me, to mark men in their sundry stations,
(255) I see nearly all living in the way I will set forth below.
They use their idle tongues, too ready to move their lips,
Yet their arms are slow to act and lag behind their words.
When there is no consistency between speeches and actions,
Is it not obvious who must perforce bear the consequences?
When the hour of judgment comes, it will be too late then
To grind their teeth for remorse, ah, many hours too late.

128. A set of men I know who differ from others of their race,
(258) In that they hold in total scorn both justice and reason.
Relying solely on their own cleverness, and nothing else,
Through tortuous dialectics, they reach evil conclusions.
If I tell them to curb their speech, they feign deafness.
When I whip them with my reproof, they turn away from me.
As for me, I do not mind at all if they amend their ways,
But I know so well they are hastening their own downfall.

129.   A handsome man I know who brings profound pity to my heart.
(259) An excellent poet he is, and spends his days in deep quiet.
       He has mastered the old style of the Han and Wei dynasties.
       In the new style, he equals the poets of the T'ang dynasty.
       Tapestry-like, words are woven into sentences by his brush.
       He has the incredible skill to present startling novelties.
       Alas, he lacks power to depict the scenes of his own heart.
       All his beautiful words have proved but a stupendous waste.

130.   A solitary crane flies sublime, athwart the boundless sky.
(260) Wild sparrows swarm to sunny hedges, forming noisy flocks.
       Horned dragons shroud themselves in fathomless whirlpools.
       Playful monkeys flit about, high above on tapering boughs.
       All living things, large and small, have their own places,
       Suitable to their individual nature, active or stationary.
       Treat an albatross to the lavish feast intended for a man;
       It might find the fare dainty, but never truly satisfying.

131.   I have seen both court and country in my long wanderings.
(262) Both court and country I now find much as they once were.
       How I wish I could say men as well have not altered much.
       Few I now find who live as upright as those who perished.
       It hardly matters whether one is clothed in black or not;
       Everyone is courting self-destruction one way or another.
       Once beaten bare, the broad highway of faith lies untrod,
       Rank grass coming up here and there to block the passage.

132.   The harvest done, the field is left for the noisy crickets.
(264) Piles of straw set aflame, the hamlet is filled with smoke.
       The hearths are lit, and farmers spend their long evenings,
       Plaiting straw mats, getting ready so soon for next spring.
       The whole house sits together amid loud cackles and laughs.
       No one opens his mouth to lie, nor any to defend his truth.
       Totally unlike these farmers are the residents of the city;
       They must bend their knees, pleading, against their desire.

133.
(266)
All the three regions of Etsu province teem with beauties.
They have gathered by the greenest river for a merry ball.
From their heads slant down hairpins, trimmed with pearls;
Their skirts fly, to reveal their rose-coloured underwear.
They nip budding grass to make garlands for young princes.
They cut flowering twigs, while flirting with noble lords.
Alas, this joyous scene with all its charms stays a trice.
Just so long these beauties live to sing, drink and dance.

134.
(269)
How brightly arrayed they are, these women of a gay house.
How artfully they speak, how joyfully they beam in smiles.
All day, they court the lords and princes passing by them.
They dance upon a bank, to the east of the greenest river.
Their treble songs draw the soul out of a chance listener.
Their airy steps and backward glances blind the observers.
Alas, gloom descends on them as it does on all the others.
Shortly, they will stand in the wind, rubbing their necks.

135.
(271)

On Midsummer Festival Day

My mother had been dead some years when my father departed.
A misfortune is most likely to be followed by a misfortune.
My mother's two sisters were alive, when I lost my parents.
The elder sister was called Myōgo and the younger, Myōshin.
Myōshin embarked on her solitary journey last year, in May.
Myōgo' was still alive last year, on Midsummer Festival Day.
A year later, on the same day, I find her gone past recall.
Alas, she, too, has become a resident of the eternal gloom.
Last year, I was in Kyōto, and shed my tears for my father,
And I have wandered away this year to this lake-side house.
The farther away I go, the more I think of my dead parents,
Though I rove along, south to north, like a wandering leaf.
Now I pick herbs by the Ki river, every hour and every day,
And with my wet eyes, see the banks stretching to Mt. Kōya.
It was there, I attended the Midsummer Festival a year ago.
Red banners flying, the priests chanted on the holy ground.
A fresh breeze came blowing from the surrounding mountains,

And drove away from our hearts the heavy dust of the world.
Then, after a shower, in the sombre shadow of a bashō tree,
I thought I had seen the souls of the departed, revisiting.
They all had taken so much pleasure in the sacred ceremony,
And accepted the honour accorded to them with blissful joy.
Now I urge you, sweet souls, to find your everlasting rest,
Swiftly crossing the river of time to the land of eternity.

136.
(272)
A drink with Yoshiyuki, my greatest pleasure

Seldom have two brothers a chance to meet, as we have done.
Both of us now have a touch of frost in our drooping brows.
However, let us take genuine delight in the world at peace
And drink together day to day, till we both lose ourselves.

137.
(273)
To Master Shiyō, my former teacher

At the foot of a rough hill, there lies an old gravestone.
Round it, rank weeds grow taller and thicker year by year.
Not a relative is left to spray water over the sealed urn.
Woodcutters alone pass by it, casting but cold eyes on it.
I was once a pupil at his school, a boy with hanging hair.
How I followed him, played with him, by the Narrow Stream.
One morning I took my leave, to depart on my solitary way,
And years have passed while we both lived in deep silence.
Today, I have returned here to find him laid in the grave.
Ah, how could I honour with due respect his departed soul?
Sprinkling but a handful of purified water over his stone,
I say my earnest prayers for his repose in life hereafter.
Meanwhile, the sun on its course went apace behind a hill,
And left me alone amid the howling roar of the dark pines.
I went away many times, each time but to retrace my steps,
Till at last my sleeves were quite soaked in my own tears.

138.
(275)
On the death of Yukinori

Our life span, however long, lasts not for a hundred years,
And we all drift along through time like a boat in a river.
Our course has been determined by Karma, a chain of causes.
Few of us, though, are wise enough to take it into account.
When I was a boy, I had a couple of close friends about me.
We often played together on the banks of the Narrow Stream.
Already, literature was our concern, and we often sat down
In an earnest conversation, not caring how time crept away.
Among my friends, you were closest to me, and knew me best.
We went to school together, studied under the same teacher.
Many a morning, we followed each other on our way to class,
And having arrived, we sat down on the floor, side by side.
One day, however, a storm rose out of the dark to sever us.
We were then parted from each other, like heaven and earth.
You had in your mind a deep aspiration for worldly dignity.
I had in my heart a secret longing to follow ancient sages.
You went eastward, taking yourself beyond the Capital City.
I journeyed west to a holy temple in a province by the sea.
The west, however, was not my home, where I truly belonged.
Therefore, I tarried but a few seasons, and left the place.
After years of aimless wandering, I have at last come home,
Though I still live in the mountains under drifting clouds.
I seek shelter in a cottage, covered with a roof of pampas,
Standing apart halfway up on a shadowy slope of Mt. Kugami.
The home, however, is not the home I used to know long ago.
Each morning and every night, some change occurs somewhere.
Some time ago I met an acquaintance and inquired after you.
Instead of replying, he pointed out a grassy hillock to me.
When I knew what it was, my breath stopped, and I was dumb.
After moments of silence, tears swelled in spite of myself.
Once on a time, you were my bosom friend, studying with me.
Now you are imprisoned in a grave beneath the mossy ground.
It was my daily comfort to listen to your honeyed speeches.
Alas, we are now separated for ever as darkness from light.
How appallingly transitory are the three divisions of time!
How strangely undefinable are the six steps of our journey!
I took leave of the aged man who had told me of your death,

And walked out of the city on my cane, away from the noise.
On each side of the highway rose a line of evergreen pines,
And beyond them, roofs of large temples pierced the clouds.
Willow trees boasted of the flags fluttering in the breeze,
And roadside peaches dropped their flowers on gilt saddles.
For it was a market day, and busy swarms thronged the city,
And people marched along the highroad in a long procession.
I watched them with a steady gaze, cherishing a faint hope.
Alas, tears blinded my sight when I found no familiar face.

139. (278) Two Poems

*On hearing a sermon by Ugan at a layman's home
In the City of Niigata during my begging round*

Sir, you are like a butcher who hangs out a sheep's head
To boost the sale of the dog meat he hides in the corner.
Yet I cannot but ask myself, why was it I sought you out
So madly, unless I cherished in my heart your foul smell?

I am known as an utterly useless man, lazy beyond remedy.
I walk along from one place to another, begging for food.
At last I have met you amidst the roar of a crowded city.
We have enjoyed a broad laugh and found our mutual peace.

140. (280) *On visiting Ugan's cottage*

The wicket is locked, and silence holds the grassy cottage.
Out of the hollow autumn sky, leaves come down in a shower.
Sparrows have formed a large bevy, and twitter on the roof.
Evening glow fills with after-warmth the neglected village.
I have come over hills and rivers, hoping to see you alone,
Trusting myself to my crooked cane, as in my former visits.
In a twinkling, however, time deprives us of what we prize,
As a torrent carries everything away, leaving but a murmur.

141. (284)

Saichi, my friend, is truly a man worthy of my best praise.
A great pity it is, few alive know the reach of his wisdom.

Once he chanced to write for me an ode in honour of Buddha.
Never can I see it without soaking my sleeves in hot tears.

142.
(287)
To Saichi

To visit my holy teacher on his deathbed, I closed my gate,
And walked many a mile, with just a flask in my aging hand.
I saw a waterfowl flying far beyond the stretch of the sea,
And around me, hills aglow in their last colours of autumn.

143.
(289)
Shortly after the death of Saichi

On this dark, drizzling day, in the dreadful month of June,
Where have you gone, I wonder, leaving me lingering behind?
Hoping to cure my loneliness, I have come to your old home,
But in the greenest hills cuckoos alone raise a loud noise.

144.
(291)
On dreaming of Saichi

Twenty years after your death, you and I have met once more,
Beside a rustic bridge, in a breeze, beneath the misty moon.
Hand in hand, we walked along, talking loudly to each other,
Till we both came, unawares, to the village shrine at Yoita.

145.
(293)
The poem I made on my sick bed sounds thinner than the cricket.
I cannot make out why there is so much breach of harmony in it.
Whatever I may do, Dainin is no more to be found in this world.
Alas, no man alive now can defend my poems from grim cavillers.

146.
(294)
Daiten is a priest who has mastered the art of quiet breathing.
Oft I met him at his temple, and found joy in our conversation.
Once we were separated in Kyōto, each following his lonely way.
No news has reached me since of where he lives or what he does.

147.
(295)
Shichisei is an old friend, who rode a bamboo horse with me.
Our mutual respect has remained unchanged through the years.
Poor he is now, as he was then, when he was but my playmate.
Nonetheless bravely has he kept up the honour of his family.

148.
(296)
Long friendship is a thing that never gets quite forgotten.
On my cane, I visit my friend, Chikkyū, at his rustic home.
In the greenest foliage, amid the smoky rain of wet summer,
A big peony is ready to blaze in flames of deepest scarlet.

149.
(300)

To Chikkyū on his visit

Listen, my friend, to the cicadas singing to the waterfalls.
Look how the shower of the night has washed the world clean.
Although I have none of the good things on my kitchen table,
I can treat you, if you like, to a windowful of healthy air.

150.
(305)

To Shukumon

*Who kindly sent me a parcel of potatoes
And pears on the second day of December*

I walked up the hillside, hoping to collect some firewood.
By the time I returned home, the sun had sunk in the west.
Upon the shelf beneath my window, I was surprised to find
A parcel of potatoes and pears placed there in my absence.
The pears were wrapped, the potatoes packed in fine grass.
Attached to the parcel was a slip of paper showing a name.
Living in the hills, I always find it hard to feed myself,
Especially in winter, when I get only turnips for my fare,
So I lost no time in boiling the potatoes with bean paste.
The potatoes ran down my dry throat like a flood of honey.
I was at last satisfied when I consumed the third helping
Though I much regretted the absence of wine and my friend.
I carefully stored in a cupboard what remained in the pot,
And took a walk, revolving in my heart what to do with it.
Then I remembered an important day was due six days later,

When it was proper to honour my altar with some offerings,
If the supporters of my belief brought me anything, be it
A borrowing from another temple or a purchase in the city.
But the fact was, with all their fortunes thrown together,
My followers could not buy a basketful at December prices.
Well, we have at least the generous gift of my old friend.
We can stand the Saint of the West a rich feast this year.
Should anyone care to know more about it, let me tell him
Pears will accompany tea, and potatoes will be boiled hot.

A defence of Fujie, a physician

151. *A poem written in his person*
(307) I am by nature slow in all things to learn worldly prudence.
For this reason, I have found peace, living as I do in town.
I apply moxa to men's flesh and live modestly on the income.
Having naught else to do, I face a checkerboard all my life.

To Suzuki Ryūzō

152.
(309) Last summer, on one of those hectic days when heat burns all,
I found myself ill, my limbs numb, my stomach unable to hold.
I had strange visions, ghastly visitors from dreamy darkness.
For three long days, neither drink nor food passed my throat.
Then, your kind gift, a good remedy, reached me unexpectedly.
Powder so fine, so sweet in colour and smell, I had not seen.
I sat upright and with a bow of reverence, I took the powder.
It wrought a marvel in me, sending life through all my veins.

To Suzuki Chinzō, on his return from a journey

153. *A poem written in his person*
(311) I have just returned from my wandering to far-off provinces.
All the ninety days of autumn spent, heaven shuts exhausted.
Should anyone crave to ascertain how far I went, travelling,
Come, I shall teach you by these calluses covering my soles.

154. *An evening visit with Jakusai at his cottage*
(316) My house broken, my family dispersed, I went away from home.
I have rambled since, south to north, north to south, alone.
This evening I walk again on a village road, as it drizzles,
For no other purpose than to seek you out, swinging my cane.

155. *A reply to a friend*
(319) A blazing candle in my hand, I sit down with you one night.
The Tempestuous Window is calm tonight, snow softly flying.
We both feel quite at ease and our hearts unite in harmony.
Neither of us minds at all rights and wrongs here on earth.

156. *To the nun Ikei in Edo on December twenty-fifth*
(323) In search of the holy texts, complete and most stupendous,
You have abandoned your home, and slave amid alien people.
Having met you, I am at a loss what to say to comfort you.
In this bitter weather, pray look after yourself.

157. *To the master of a house*
(324) A few poems I have composed since I came here.
I have them in rough drafts for lack of money.
Fair copies I want to make, and send them to Shūbi, if I may.
Good man, let me beg of you a gift of some paper and a brush.

158. Hōsai is an extraordinary man, armed with a brave spirit.
(325) For reasons beyond my reach, he rambled out to this area.
I came upon him yesterday amid the roar of a market city.
Our hands cemented, we both choked ourselves in laughter.

159.
(326)
To the priests Jizen and Nisen
On their visit to my house

My cottage is situated in the low foothills of Mt. Kugami.
Throw a window open, and rows of mountains front our eyes.
If you happen to like the hushed loneliness of this place,
I pray you to visit my sheltered gate time and time again.

160.
(327)
Stopping by the house of the priest Ichigyō

One quiet day in autumn, I have wandered out of my cottage,
Without a single escort, trusting myself to a crooked cane.
Red berries of wild goumi are the sole colour in the hills.
The cold river goes its way through yellow leaves of reeds.
I cross a bridge, the same I have walked across many times.
I sit in a house, the same I know well from my past visits.
But this ghastly blast that sweeps in the descending gloom
And the fatal hollow of the house are more than I can bear.

161.
(329)
On visiting the Cloud Promontory
With the priest Tenge in autumn

This life of ours is so unstable that we flit through it
Like rootless seaweeds drifting to and fro on every tide.
Who can indeed safely trust his heart to things so frail?
It was, therefore, not without cause, nor without reason,
That I took leave of my parents, swinging my belled cane,
And marched away from my city, waving my hands to my kin.
Since then, I have kept beside me a gown full of patches
And a bowl that has sustained my flesh for many a spring.
By what seems to me but a chance, I have found rest here,
And live in a grassy house, dreaming of final fulfilment.
In you, I have found a congenial spirit, so tied in love,
That we do not know which of us is the host or the guest.
At this promontory, the wind blows high amid lofty pines,
And frost lies cold on the last few chrysanthemum blooms.
You and I join hands together, our thoughts above clouds,
Quite oblivious of what we are, standing on a wild shore.

162. *To Issairō*
(330) Early in the morning, one of those burning days in summer,
I sought shelter from the heat, high at a mountain temple.
In hushed solitude, by the parapet of an elevated terrace,
A gentle breeze from the pine woods fanned my sacred gown.
It was not long, as it seemed, before I saw birds go home
Amid the whole range of mountain peaks aglow with the sun.
I also dragged my feet down the slope upon my bamboo cane,
And slipped into my grassy house at a most leisurely pace.
A spray of yellow leaves arrested me in front of a window,
And by a short poem tied to it, I discovered to my regret
That you had paid an unrewarded visit in my short absence.
For hours after that, sweet thoughts of you so whelmed me
That at last I took my brush and wrote this poem on a fan.
Kindly accept it, my friend, a poor meed for your journey.

163. *Stopping by the house of Sekizaemon After the tea house at Kuma no Mori*
(331) For years, I have known you as a precious drinking friend.
How many times we have passed our cordial cups between us.
Today, I sought you again, but missed you by the fireside.
Brown leaves alone come dancing down to mock my dim sight.

164. *To the priest Keizan at his temple, Ganjōji*
(332) Ganjōji is situated to the west of the village of Hokkedō.
It stands by a rocky stream, half-buried in a cloudy mist.
Moss grows thick in the footpaths, barring human approach.
In the garden pond, old beyond telling, scaly fishes leap.
Upon the mountain ridges, lofty pines reach the sunny sky.
Farther away, Mt. Yahiko presents its majestic silhouette.
One day in September, led by fair weather, I gave a knock
At your gate, totally unpremeditated, on my begging round.
I am a priest living beyond the pale of things and events.
Likewise, you are free, sworn unto the peace of the heart.
We sat together a whole day, nothing disturbing our quiet,
Except the drinks, the cliffs, our laughs, our own voices.

165.
(333)
Priest Senkei is a sacred man, seeker after mysterious truth.
Mute he works, his lips locked in silence.
For thirty years, he has laboured under Priest Kokusen,
Never sitting in a temple, nor reading holy texts,
Not even saying a word of prayer in audible voice.
Vegetables he grows, giving them free to the villagers.
I saw him once, never seeing him in his true self,
Met him once, never knowing him.
Now I pine after him, hoping to follow him in my humble ways.
Priest Senkei is a sacred man, seeker after mysterious truth.

166.
(334)
An improvisation

For hours, since I sat facing you, you have stayed mute.
Your meaning, ampler than words, addresses itself to me.
Cases removed, books lie open, scattered by the bedside.
Beyond the bamboo screen, a shower falls on a plum tree.

167.
(337)
Walking with my friend under the moon

On this spring night, the moon shines through silver haze.
You and I walk along, hand in hand, at our lingering pace.
Our smallest whisper must have shaken them in the silence:
The ducks fly away all at once, beating their light wings.

168.
(343)
A singular stroke of luck graced my bag with a copper coin;
Therefore, I have sought your presence, my sleeping dragon.
Though I have long cherished the idea of drinking with you,
I have not had the luck of finding a coin in my bag before.

169.
(344)
Bird songs reach me piecemeal, a riot of blossoms on earth.
I opened my cottage gate moments ago to give you a welcome.
The setting sun lingers on the mossy ground in a soft wind.
Riming, chins in our hands, we think beyond time and space.

170.   A magnificent temple towers to heaven by the Eternal Bridge.
(347) Priests rival in its halls the sermons of rocks and streams.
       I, for one, would gladly sacrifice my brows for my brethren,
       But I fear I might aggravate the war, already rank as weeds.

         A reply to my friend's letter
171.
(350) A short walk will take me from here to your smoky village.
       Yet the sleet has fixed me all the morning before my desk.
       Hardly a night, as it seems, since we talked about poetry,
       But already twenty stormy days stand between now and then.
       I dip my brush in a pool of ink, to copy the perfect hand
       Of the holy book you lent me, oft sighing for my weakness.
       Take this poem as my solemn pledge for the call I owe you.
       Soon as ice goes, I will swing my cane down the mossy way.

172.   Since I began to seek discipline at the temple, Entsūji,
(351) Many winters and springs have I known in abject poverty.
       In front of the gate stands a town of a thousand houses
       Where I have not a relative, nor a friend, to assist me.
       I wash with my own hands the clothes covered with filth,
       And allay my hunger, begging for alms from door to door.
       All this is because I read in a chronicle of old saints
       That poverty was once prized by Sōka more than anything.

173.   Under the roof of the Entsūji temple, I often complained
(352) Of my utter solitude, my isolation from others around me.
       Bent under a pile of firewood, I yearned for noble Hō'on.
       Turning a treadmill, I sought to imitate old Enō at work.
       I seated myself in a lecture room before anyone else did.
       I rose from bed earlier than any for the morning service.
       One fatal day, however, I left the temple at my own whim,
       Now thirty long years ago, as I look back upon my course.
       A mass of mountains and a whirl of waves separate me now,
       So that no news of the holy temple reach my anxious ears.
       Fully aware of what I owe to my teacher, I sit by myself,
       Shedding remorseful tears to the moaning river before me.

174.
(354) On a hill behind the Entsūji temple stands a shady forest.
Drinking, I sat with you one summer day, to shun the heat.
We emptied our cask to the last drop before we made poems.
So protected, we sat there till the curfew closed the day.

175.
(356)
In protest to the priest Shakuan
Against his notice of prohibition
At Entsūji

Seven times have I known frost in the seven years of tramping.
I now find my former hourglass lifeless, its water nearly dry.
Who will have mercy now upon the thirsty souls under the roof?
After my pious bow, I yearn for the old days prohibition-free.

176.
(357)
Hearing a cuckoo in my wandering

Springtide has returned, but I have no place to return to.
The cuckoo alone shouts to me, as if it could coo me home.
Danger lurks everywhere, so long as we live on this earth,
But when will it be possible for me to find peace at home?

177.
(361)
On my way to Mt. Kōya, I found myself penniless

A bowl and a flask in my hand, I walk any distance, begging,
But what can I do in spring when my gown is torn to tatters?
I know full well I have not a single coin in my begging bag.
No doubt, I have erred, misled by the magic power of Nature.

178.
(362)
Two poems in the heavy rain
On my way to the Ise shrine

Since I left the capital city of Kyōto, I have travelled
For a fortnight but two days, as I count with my fingers.
All this while, not a day excepted, it poured so heavily
That I drew up these meagre lines to express my sympathy
For the wild geese, beating their wet wings in the cloud,
And the wayside peach trees, drooping their red branches,

And the boatmen risen to see the river banks washed away,
And the travellers, groping at night for their lost ways.
My own journey has more than half its way still unwalked,
And I am arrested here, my brows knit, my eyes cast down.
Last year in the autumn, a rebellious storm fell upon us,
Blasting pestilent breath for three days without a break,
Pulling sturdy trees out of their long accustomed mounds,
Blowing thatched roofs far beyond the rain-lashed clouds,
And sending the rice price above the reach of common men.
The long rain will likewise bring affliction this spring,
And if it does not stop, even while I am despairing thus,
What will the farmers do, to avoid their own destruction?

Forced by the heavy rain, I sought an overnight shelter,
In despair, here by a faltering lamp in a broken temple.
What use is it now to dry my wet clothes for travelling?
Better it were to lie down and ease myself with singing.
The rain beating in my tired ears all through the night,
I remained awake, my pillow forsaken, till another dawn.

179.
(364)
Sick at Itoigawa on a rainy day on my way home

Nothing but a gown and a bowl on me, I have wandered long.
Here I am taken ill still on my road, and to nurse myself
I sit by a window, one night, an incense burner before me.
The rain urges me to think about my ten years on the road.

180.
(365)
The Zenkōji temple revisited

Once before, I visited this place, led by my sacred teacher,
Already twenty long years ago, as I look back upon the past.
The stream before the gate and the rows of mountains behind,
With all their sublime beauty, are still as I once saw them.

CHINESE POEMS

181.
(366)
On my way to Yonezawa

The last of the geese head south, flying in lonely flocks.
I am aware of the autumn stretching all the way before me.
The mountains are stripped of leaves after the icy shower.
Far away, a village lies asleep, lit by the declining sun.

182.
(367)
At night at the post-town of Tamagawa

The wind drives the rain at night, already past mid-autumn.
A traveller am I, my heart heavy with the ills of the road.
Often, during the long night, my uneasy dream is disturbed
By the moaning river, taken by me for the howl of the rain.

183.
(368)
One autumn morning
By the parapet of the Fragrant Pavilion

Granted a night's lodging here at this temple last night,
I rise early to bow in reverence before the lotus throne.
A solitary light burning bright in the gloom of the hall,
Everything seems to have found its home in the stillness.
The temple bell clangs loud, all of a sudden, five times,
And its profound echoes awake trees and lakes from sleep.
The eastern sky is already touched by the white sunlight,
But the sky above is dark and void after the rainy night.
In mid-autumnal cool, at the turn of August to September,
A morning breeze gives the whole scene bracing crispness.
By and by, lingering mists gather themselves in the dale,
And the mountaintops glow in the beams of the bright sun.
Now a lofty tower is seen rising into the once empty sky,
And the roof of the main building looms behind the trees.
Down the craggy cliff, rash and fierce, leaps a cataract,
Its foaming waves and driving sprays flying up to heaven.
Farther away, men and women are seen thronging the wharf,
And ferryboats are busy, racing one another in the river.
The shores and beaches lie half-hidden in a veil of mist,
And distant cedars and cypresses afford a feast of green.
For years now, I have been a lonely pilgrim, self-exiled,

Walking from one place to another to follow the ancients.
Not until this fine morning, however, have I seen a view,
Such as this, whose beauty is beyond man's reach to tell.
Scents they must have taken from the land of the blessed,
And brought them here, to perfume this Fragrant Pavilion.
In its chaste morning air, almost oblivious of what I am,
I make this poem by myself, and recite it to my own ears.
Yet as a pilgrim, I have ahead of me miles of dusty road,
And the thoughts of the long journey make my heart heavy.
All men are subject to decay, and once I fly this temple,
Will it be possible for me to return and enjoy its quiet?
Half-striving to depart, yet totally unable to walk away,
I stand confounded, my crooked cane firm against the sod.

184. One night, at the end of a road lined with black houses,
(373) Together with a poor doting woman, I chanted holy texts.
Blame me not, friends, for blotting myself thus in soot.
How many more nights, truly, am I granted here on earth?

185. *To an orchis flower*
(378) In the deepest recess of a narrow valley stands a beauty.
In her serenity, unequalled; unrivalled in her sweetness.
She heaves a soft sigh, as if she were pining for a mate,
All alone in a quiet shade beneath a tall bamboo thicket.

186. The volume of Kanzan's poetry in my house, I esteem more
(380) Than the sacred sutras or countless commentaries on them.
A brush in hand, I have made copies on my bedside screen,
And now and then, I brood on them, feasting on each poem.

187. One brilliant day in fair May, I saw on a silver stream
(385) A painted barge towed upstream with a young lady aboard.
She held in her soft fingers the glory of a lotus plant,
The white of her skin vying with the pink of the flower.

A bright youth came riding at a trot along the causeway.
Under a rare-green willow tree, he came to a standstill
And, speechless, so fixed his gaze upon the lady afloat,
He betrayed, unawares, the fire gnawing his inward self.

188. A noble youth I happened to see one fair day in a street.
(386) Not less than a god he seemed to me in his graceful form.
He passed by me, holding a jewel-bright whip in his hand;
Mounted on horseback, he trotted away, brushing a willow.
Above him, a young lady was looking down into the street.
She plucked at the strings of her harp beside her window,
And chased with her eyes the young man in the sunny dust,
All the way until he faded on the endless road to Shinpō.

189. A maid there was not far from the town where I was born.
(387) She had the fame of being the finest bloom in the place.
A youth in an eastern village courted her every morning.
A noble lad in a western village sought her every night.
Again and again they wrote her letters of honeyed words,
And over and over they sent her gifts of infinite value.
Thus time slipped by—many winters of frost and snow,
The maiden herself unable to decide which man to choose.
She could not favour one man without grieving the other.
She could not love them both without hurting her honour.
One day at length she gave herself to a bottomless gulf.
Bitter fate it was that she thus had to refuse both men!

190. When I was no more than a boy, I strolled about the city,
(389) Always seeking pleasure in the most flourishing quarters.
I dressed myself up in a soft downy vest of duck feather,
And I often mounted a brown horse with a snow-white face.
In the morning, I rode out to entertain myself at Shinpō.
At twilight, I fed my eyes on the peach blossoms at Kayō.
I returned late, caring not a straw where to rest myself.
Questioned, I turned with a smile to a house of ill fame.

191. Two brothers I know among my companions of my native town.
(391) Of the same blood as they are, they disagree in character.
One of them is clever in action and mellifluous in speech.
The other is slow in response and awkward in conversation.
But it seems right beyond doubt, as I regard the slow one,
That it is he who has more leisure than anyone can afford,
Whereas the clever one runs his busy race without a break,
Hastening from place to place, achieving nothing of worth.

192. Within the limits of my cottage I have a cat and a mouse.
(392) They are enemies, though they are both of the hairy kind.
The cat is plump, and sleeps comfortably in the sunshine.
The mouse is starved, and hunts in the darkness of night.
A darling of fortune, the cat is endowed with an ability
Wherewith it can ambush and catch numerous living things.
The mouse is doomed to its misery for its criminal habit
Of intruding into the house and breaking cherished wares.
Broken vessels, however, can be replaced at a small cost.
There is no way of restoring living things to life again.
If you, therefore, weigh the plump cat against the mouse,
Surely, the balance will betray the gravity of its crime.

193. *A reply to Jakusai's poem on my cracked bowl*
(393) One fine morning, I struck out on the road all by myself.
The hem of my skirt tucked up, I marched to an east hill,
Where, probing a thicket with my cane, I found this bowl,
And taking it up from the grass, I washed it in a stream.
Every morning, my incense lit, I eat my porridge from it.
From it I savour my soup or taste my rice in the evening.
Somewhat cracked and far from perfect in form and colour,
I know full well I have inherited it from a noble source.

194. *To my holy mace made of horn*
(394) Too precious to be thrown away in a heap of useless trash,
I hold it ever in my hand, prizing it higher than a jewel,

More glittering than the horns of a sable-armoured dragon;
Far more than the tusks of a rare-blue elephant, luminous.
It follows me on autumn nights to wherever I go preaching,
And on spring days it stays around me while I rest asleep.
Most unavailing in sweeping this-worldly dust off my head,
It serves as a whip and a cheer in my hours of discipline.

195. Monkeys are often seen picking lice on top of fiery Asama,
(395) And men striving to catch whales in the pools of the Usui.
Wrapped in a hempen dress, my skull covered like a hermit,
Why not leap about, beating my bowl and swinging my bells.
If anyone probes me for what I am, I will shout in return,
Out on the sandy beach of Suma, known as a gull's brother,
I rake salty seaweeds together and, blowing, build a fire,
So I can celebrate my empty paunch and the world at peace.

196. Many years ago, there rose to heaven a lofty paulownia tree,
(397) In the covert nook of Mt. Konron in the land of the blessed.
Its upper leaves were nursed by the beams of the rising sun,
Its roots striking a thousand feet deep into the firm earth.
A minister came one day, the Emperor's message in his hands.
Thus, the tree was felled, and of its wood, a harp was made,
An instrument, never to be surpassed in its graceful finish.
Plucked by a master, it drowned the ears in its sweet music.
A divine harmony ruled its full compass from bass to treble
And its tonal beauty ravished the heart with chaste ecstasy.
For years now, this harp has slept in the Imperial treasury,
Guarded by its gilt walls, but with none to awaken its soul,
Its scarlet strings hanging loose in the hollow of the room,
And its inlaid surface buried deep in a heap of piling dust.
Below the autumn moon that returns every year to the garden,
And under the canopy of gay blossoms that bloom each spring,
This harp has been mute, though none were forbidden its use.
It must be that no masters alive can inspire its full scope.
After the departure of Hakuga and Enryō years and years ago
No one among us now can unlock the secret of this holy harp.

197. One silent night, within the walls of my grassy cottage
(400) I sat by myself, and awakened to life the cordless harp.
The music rose to heaven, flying above the murky clouds.
It also went down the gentle river to timeless eternity.
The entire valley about me was satiate with its harmony,
And the surrounding cliffs and woods rich in its echoes.
Strangely, no one could hear the sweet music of my harp
Unless he had both his mortal ears stopped all the time.

198.   *Buddha's return to the world*
(403) This is the road he travelled in his escape from the world.
This is the road he travelled upon his return to the world.
In going and coming we must march along this sacred avenue
Through life and death, shiny false flowers on either side.

199. Wise Monju sits upright, a fierce lion below him subdued.
(404) Merciful Fugen is seated on the back of a white elephant.
Artful Myō'on transforms himself into an inlaid pedestal.
Learned Yuima lies stretched on the cushion of his couch.

200. At crossroads and in streets, a Hotei bore his sad bag
(405) Year after year, and yet at the return of another year.
None, alas, has known the endless beauty of this tramp.
Let him go home now to heaven, where he really belongs.

201. Nansen is an aged priest with a wit sharper than a drill.
(408) By what seems a sheer whim he dallied long at his temple.
By fusing his own tears with some drops of a cat's blood
He brightened the dawn of a glorious spring day at Chiyō.

202. Woman of women, she shone forth, her name being Brightest.
(409) Every morning as a peddler she took her pannier to a city.
I know not whose hand had so much skill to paint her here,
Divine above the reach of the world in her supreme beauty.

CHINESE POEMS

203.
(410)
Seeing a picture of Kōchi Hō'in

With an age-old cane, battered to its core by nightly rain,
And a gown threadbare like the fading veil of morning mist,
Stands an aged man, whoever has a sight penetrating enough
To see him in his real self, a breath in everlasting pines.

204.
(411)
Ebisu and Daikoku

I threw aside my golden hammer, and you, your fishing rod,
Having come together one singular day by a stroke of luck.
Neither you nor I knew for sure what it was we were doing.
Perhaps we meant to establish, old is old, and new is new.

205.
(412)
To a self-righting Daruma

Thrown to the earth for toy, or ridiculed by a loud sneer,
Not for a single instant he overcasts his cloudless heart.
If we could likewise fly beyond the pale of earthly fears
We should have, living on earth, a source of infinite joy.

206.
(413)
Michizane in China

Whose work is it, this perfect sketch of divine Michizane?
With the glow of sweet plum and the glory of lasting pine?
Precise in each detail is the Chinese court suit he wears.
By this all shall know him a god everywhere in this world.

207.
(414)
None before him could possibly have stood equal unto him.
None after him will be great enough to stand by his side.
Ah, Bashō, ah, Bashō, you tower so high,
One thousand years from now men will have to worship you.

208. *To the loyal forty-seven*
(415) Compelled to choose between life and death, many have erred.
Never before have I known a band like the loyal forty-seven.
One in thought, one in action, they have performed the feat,
For ever to be adored as the flower of the years of Genroku.

209. *At a monument to a virtuous woman*
(416) Her mother-in-law at leisure, she toiled in a summer field.
In winter, she waited on her mother-in-law by the fireside.
The Shōgun decreed that Professor Rin blazon in every nook
The virtue of this woman who lived at the Cloud Promontory.

210. *To the image of Tu Fu*
(417) Friend of flowers, wooer of willows, he retired to Kankakei.
Mounted on a saddle, he often played the tippler for a joke.
Half-asleep, he still dreamed of himself at the royal court.
Line after line he wrote and rewrote to counsel the emperor.

211. *In praise of Li Po*
(418) Warm in an easterly wind, after a walk on the greenest lawn,
While fast asleep, stretched out in front of an empty table,
Importuned by my good host to honour his brush and ink slab,
I wrote thus, flushed like Li Po, whom I was told to praise.

212. *To Hachisuke, an untouchable*
(419) Gold and silver, pelf and position, all perish like a vision.
Gain and loss, surfeit and paucity, are void of significance.
High and low alike, sacred as well as secular, are compelled
By the fatal chain of Karma to rise and fall as they deserve.
This man was doomed to taste mud under the Bridge of Ryōgoku.
One day he threw himself into the stream to rise out of time.
Should anyone question me on his whereabouts, I should reply,
There in the shiny disk in the river, a resident of the moon.

213.
(421)
Nothing is nobler in dignity than the white fan before me.
Painted, however scantly, it will be of a secondary value.
Its blank sphere is so ripe with meaning, you can see all
Perfectly mirrored in it, flowers, moons, and high towers.

214.
(422)

In praise of Confucius

Extraordinary!
One moment, he is before me; next moment, I find him behind me.
His knowledge is the fruit of long years' self-discipline.
His countenance is smiling, his attitude humble and respectful.
None in his day could rival him, none after him will equal him.
The town of Takkō damned him for the lack of a practical skill.
Shiro was reticent, when required to explain him.
Great Confucius, ah, great Confucius, all was because
You were boundlessly great!
Some fools were among your disciples, who sought
To measure you, themselves never coming near you.

215.
(423)

In praise of Kanzan and Jittoku

Jittoku grasps in his hand a bamboo broom.
With it he sweeps his head,
Dust for ever accumulating.
Kanzan has before him a holy text to read,
Yet he can never satisfy his soul with it.
In their times, as in ours, none wished to consult them.
They lived on the cliffs of Tendai, useless as unsold goods.
What can I do now to promote their honour,
Except to endure like them till Miroku comes to judge us?

Japanese Poems

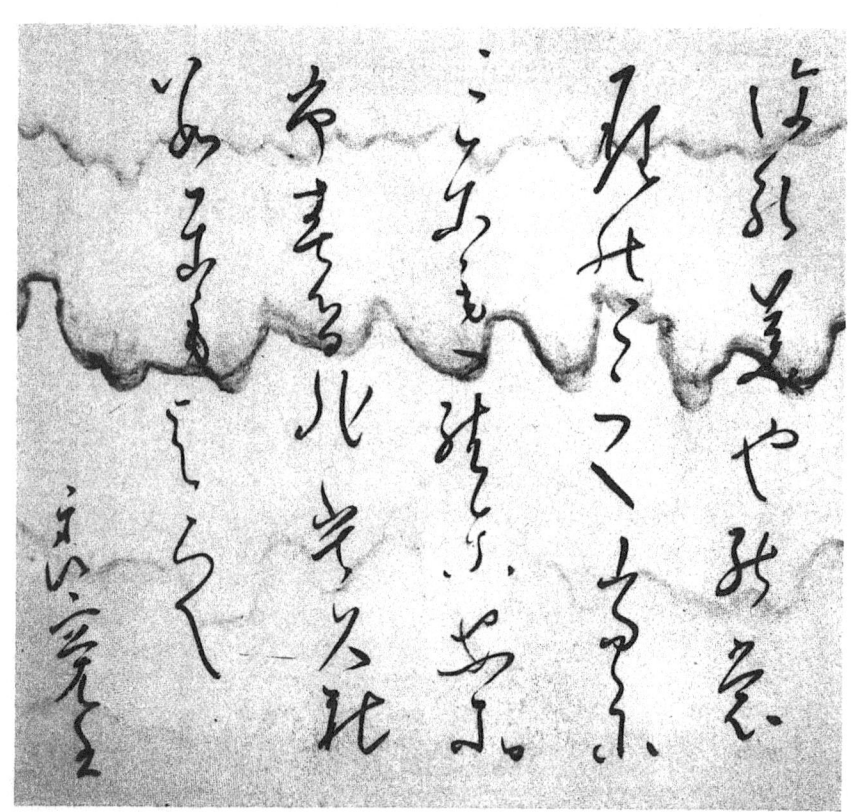

7. Japanese poem by Ryōkan (No. 217)

216. Bright as a gilt bow,
(1) Spring had come, bringing flowers.
  Begging was my aim;
I walked down the village street.
 I found on the way
Children absorbed in their sport,
 A handball bouncing.
I joined them then straight away,
 And all the long day,
One two three four five six seven,
 As they kept bouncing,
 I sang by their side,
 And as long as I sang,
 They went on bouncing.
Thus we sang, and thus we bounced,
 One misty spring day,
Sweetest of the sweet spring days,
Till darkness wrapped us complete.

 One misty spring day,
Longest of the long spring days,
 With village children,
A handball I bounced, singing,
Till gloom buried us at length.

217. In the holy shade,
(13) Beside this secluded shrine,
  Children about me,
I play one quiet spring day,
Praying the day have no end.

218. Come along, toddlers,
(17) Let's march together, shall we?
  To the mountainside.
Wait one more day, and too late
We'd reach for cherry blossoms.

219.   My old begging bowl,
(24)   Nothing else I treasure more.
      Away from its floor,
  Once my exit made from home,
      Every day at dawn,
  I have seized it in my hand.
      Every day at dusk,
  I have borne it in my palms.
      Thus at each return
  Of the thread-renewing year,
      I've kept it by me.
      Now I find it lost.
  I must have left it somewhere.
      Standing, I wonder
  How I might gain my balance.
      Seated, I know not
  Where I could settle at ease.
      Like the sea-tangle,
  My heart is tossed by fancies.
      Like the early star,
  I must start, and search it out,
      Be it in the hole
  Where toads lie in murky haunts,
      Or hidden beneath
  Those darksome clouds lingering
      Near the horizon,
  Where land and sky come together.
      Over the wet grass,
  Through the moors I must travel,
      A cane in my hand,
  Or else my cane staying here,
      In search of my bowl.
  By more than good luck, it seems,
      At this same moment
  Someone's voice rings out aloud,
      "Sir, your begging bowl,
  I have it, I've brought it here."
      Whose voice it may be,

I have not the slightest guess.
　Taking it, therefore,
For some message from the gods,
　Or for some vision
Conjured up in my sealed sleep,
　I run out to get
What I have been called to take.
　In the nick of time
It has been brought back to me,
This old begging bowl of mine.

　By the village way
I stopped for a brief moment
　To pluck violets,
And quite lost it by mistake,
The old begging bowl of mine.

　My old begging bowl
Left behind by the grassy way,
None cared enough to steal it,
None cared enough to steal it,
My prize, my old begging bowl.

220.　　　Broken begging bowl,
　　　　My old begging bowl,
Now as before, bear it high,
　　Broken begging bowl,
　　My old begging bowl,
　　Broken begging bowl,
　　My old begging bowl,
Bear it high, and go begging,
　All day and each day.

221.　　*A day of begging in Teradomari*
(33)　　Madly in pursuit,
Cod swim up and down the tide.
　　Likewise in a fuss,
　　At the break of day,

       I sweep upward along the road,
          And after sunset,
       The whole landscape quivering,
       Downward I run in great haste.

222.   Heaven and ocean
(46)   Look all but joined to my view,
          And far, far above
       The vast stretch of level sea,
       Looms Sado, rock-bound island.

223.   In the land of Tsu,
(49)   Niched deep in Takano woods,
          At an old temple,
       I bent my ears all the night
       To the cedar leaves dripping.

          At Akashi
224.
(50)   Gentle, salty wind,
       Blow softly this cold evening,
          For you will find me
       Lodged by myself in the shrine,
       Half-dreaming of ancient times.

225.   What a view it is!
(52)   And what a name for the beach,
          Waka no Ura!
       Embalmed by its balmy view,
       I take in the spring delight.

226.   Coming to Ise,
(57)   Seated on the quiet strand,
          How I long to hear
       Divine tales of ancient times
       Amid spring waves fluttering.

JAPANESE POEMS

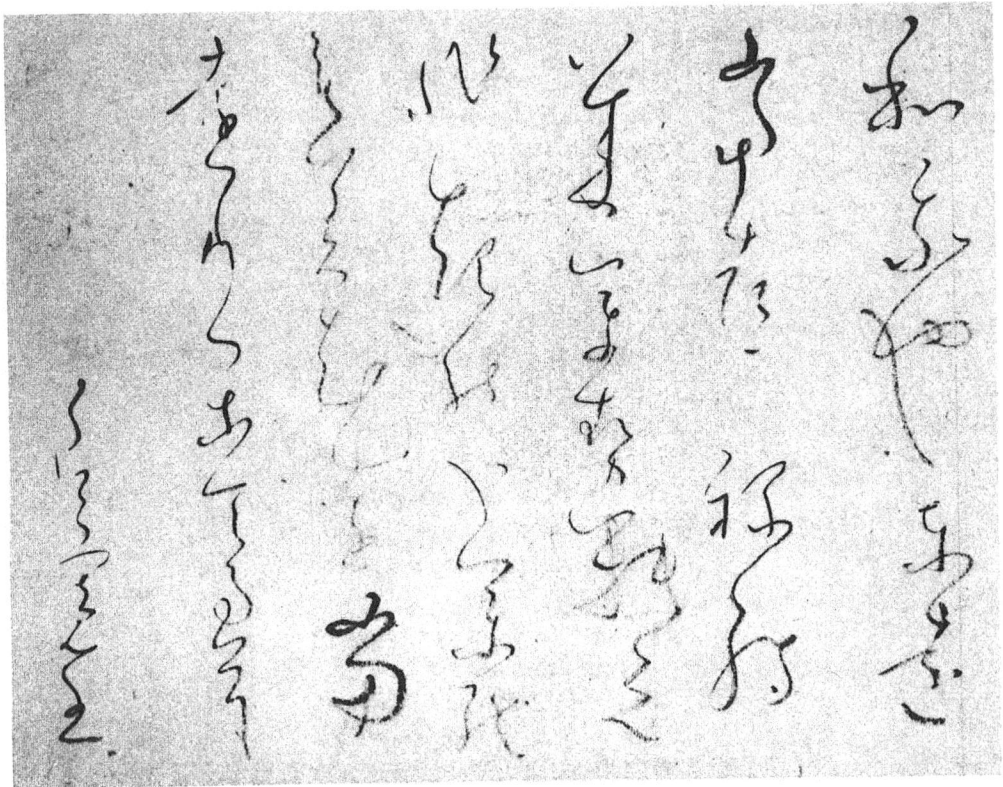

8. Japanese poem by Ryōkan (No. 233, 2nd envoy)

227.   For a thousand years,
(62)   Endless times a thousand years,
        May your highness live.
      The lush flowers of your court
      Have made me speechless with joy.

228.   There in Fukui,
(69)   By the bridge of Yatare,
        All alone I saw,
      Rain coming down from above,
      The sun shining in the sky.

229.   Homeward if you go,
(82)   Will you tell my kith and kin,
            For their own comfort,
        That at last I've walked over
        The whole stretch of Ōmi road.

230.   Foothills far below,
(1298) Mount Kugami soars to heaven.
            For its dignity,
        I hold it in great esteem.
            Upon its beauty,
        I hope to feed my eyes still.
            Down its precipice,
        Trees in thick clusters grow.
            Along its ravines,
        A pure stream runs in rapids.
            No other reason
        He must have had for himself,
            Every saint of yore,
        Who sought shelter hereabouts,
            Hoping to find peace
        With himself and with the world.
            Far be it from me
        That I should be thought one such,
            Yet never blame me
        For removing myself like them.
            This holy mountain
        Shall be my strongest defence
        Until the whole world ceases.

            Once upon a time
        A saint struck out on his way,
            Here in this mountain.
        Up the same steep way I climb,
        Though I trail far behind him.

231.   In the shady nook,
(100)   Loving the hushed quietness
              Of Mount Kugami,
          I have a while sought shelter,
          Nought but my cane beside me.

232.   By a hundred turns
(1293) I have climbed Mount Yahiko.
              To its highest peak
          I have at last brought myself.
              From its top I watch
          Eightfold clouds moving away,
              At its very feet,
          A vast sea of trees spreading.
              Along its ravines,
          Cataracts fall with whispers.
              No mountains I know
          Better than this I stand upon.
              No rapids run down
          With sounds purer than I hear.
              This is the reason
          Why a revered god has built
          His sacred home at this spot.

              Step by step I rose
          Up the shady pine-wood road
              On Mount Yahiko,
          Reaching at last its summit,
          Up the shady pine-wood road.

233.   Foothills far below,
(1276) Mount Kugami soars to heaven.
              At its shady foot
          Stands the shrine of Otogo.
              Here I live alone
          Every morning and each night
              On the rugged rocks,

  Or through the mossy footway,
   Coming and going
  To perform my daily chores.
   Before me rises,
  Each time I cast up my eyes,
   A primeval grove
  Divine in its dark grandeur.
   Every year in May,
  Cuckoos return from the south,
   And in noisy flocks
  Swell their throats in ecstasy.
   When, in September,
  Rain comes drizzling from above,
   Seated by the hearth
  I tear off bright maple leaves.
   Thus for many years,
  As long as life stays with me,
  Here I shall live free as air.

   In the shady grove,
  Hopping light from twig to twig,
   Cuckoos in a flock
  Swell their throats in ecstasy,
  Now that spring has crept away.

   Can I entice you
  To rest your feet in my house?
   Over the foothills
  Perhaps you will come gleaning
  Red maple leaves all the way.

   Frosty maple leaves
  Bright in their autumnal hues,
   And summer cuckoos,
  I shall keep in mind for years
  And years, until my life fails.

   Amid holy trees,
  Close to the Otogo shrine,
   Seated all alone
  I hear the sacred bells ring:
  Perhaps, a call from a friend.

234. At this lovely spot,
(104) Where summer grasses run wild,
   Hindered by nothing,
  I shall build a small cottage
  And seek a while my own peace.

235. On a holy ground,
(107) Beneath the revered oak tree,
   At its bulky base,
  Let me hold my place a while,
  Beneath the revered oak tree.

236. If anyone asks me
(109) Where is my home to be found,
   My reply will be,
  To the east of the fair stream
  That sweeps glowing in the sky.

237. On the mountainside,
(115) How often I've fetched firewood,
   An axe in my hand,
  And how often I've bent my ears
  To the songs of spring warblers.

238. Leaves I must gather,
(117) Water I must fetch with haste,
   And vegetables,
  This morning between the rains
  That come drizzling from above.

239. Whatever I do,
(126) I do not ply my own trade
   Or my business,
  Yet I have but a few days
  I can spend in quiet peace.

240.   In sheer idleness,
(131) I sat down upon the floor
           Of an old temple,
       And gazed vaguely before me,
       Raindrops pattering all day.

241.   All across the sky,
(146) The sun has travelled on time,
           Ready now to set.
       Many more miles I must tramp,
       Burdened with a weighty sack.

242.   Remote villages
(150) Wrapped in the gathering mist,
           Twilight descending,
       I haste along the rough road
       Toward my house, cedar-swathed.

243.   To whom can I vent
(153) My gloom on this autumn day
           As it dims away?
       In the crate placed on my back,
       I have but some blades of grass.

244.   Polar wind flying,
(157) Icy snow has started to fall.
           Snow driving along,
       Rain has begun to come down.
           In the pitchy dark,
       As I listen, pricking my ears,
           Lonely wild geese,
       All across the boundless sky,
       Strive against the elements.

In my grassy house,
Seated at ease all night long,
    I listen all alone
To the wind-shot drops of hail,
Sweeping through cedar needles.

245.   Awake at midnight,
(163) I bend my ears to the cries
    Of a lonely hart,
While feeling in my deep self,
My own loneliness past cure.

246.   Awakened at home
(168) In the small hours of morning,
    I am astonished
By the fresh-fed ridge cascade
Leaping down the massive rocks.

247.   Far in the dim town,
(175) Hollow shells are sounded often,
    Alarms blown, I fear,
As dikes collapse, swamped over
Under the weight of this storm.

248.   Mount Kugami,
(114) Some steps up its precipice,
    In the holy shade,
Close to the Otogo shrine,
    I live by myself,
Each morning and each evening,
    Up the rocky way
Climbing with a heavy burden
    To gather firewood,
Or down the steep valley way
    To draw fresh water.

Day to day, for countless days,
  Thus I have managed,
Till at length in recent years
  A sickness holds me,
And tortures me with the fear
  That I might perish,
Friendless like cicada shells,
  But few days ahead;
And that I might be laid down,
A rotten thing beneath a rock.

249.   Upon the dark night,
(181)   When will the dawn come to smile?
          Upon the dark night,
      If the pied dawn starts to smile,
          A woman will come
      And wash my foul garments clean.
          Tossing many times
      I fouled my shirts and my pants,
      Aching through the entire night.

250.   The infinite night,
(182)   Till at last the morning came,
      I had spent fouling my shirts,
          And in the daytime,
      I often dashed to the back-house
      Alas, reaching it far too late.

251.   Starved by my illness,
(184)   Not by my free choice starving,
          My stomach empty,
      I must long ease my sick bones,
      Till time lends me strength again.

252.   Beside a slow fire,
(185) I stretched out my weary legs,
         And lay on my back,
       All the time feeling the chill
       That pierced into my stomach.

253.   All things about me,
(189) Years and months not excepted,
         Come and go in time.
       Why does sick old age alone
       Creep on me, and stay with me?

254.   In Shikishima,
(455) Otherwise known as Yamato,
         Since antiquity
       Men have avoided speaking.
         Yet I am fully
       Determined to raise my voice,
         Because last summer
       A surprise present reached me
         From my good brother,
       Feathery fur of smooth touch,
         Whiter than cotton,
       Softer far than the best silk.
         Never in my house
       Had I treasured such a thing.
         Awake in daytime,
       I bore it rolled round my neck.
         Asleep at midnight,
       I stored it spread beneath me.
         Not for one moment
       Could I dream of leaving it,
       For fear it should slip away.
       Yet no marvel it performed
         Although I waited
       With patience for a long time.
         Changing my method

In deep reflection, therefore,
   I took the risk of
Wearing it beneath my shirt,
   Yes, my body shirt,
   The one I slept in,
Right next to my fleshly skin,
   And as I lay still
I was amazed by the warmth
   Of the sleep I had.
So warm was the fur, in fact,
   That at midwinter
Spring seemed to have come to me
While I stayed dreaming in bed.

   What can I send you
In return for your rare gift,
   Comparable only
With what I prize most in me,
My own life, my sole treasure?

   About me I have
Nothing proper to send you,
   But my living breath.
Yet, I warn you in good time.
Brag not about it, my friend.

255.   On a sunny day,
(458) Delving deep into thick snow,
   My beloved friend,
You must have uncovered them.
   Little lily bulbs,
   Little lily bulbs,
These little lily bulbs are
More tasty than I can praise.

256. *Three seaweed poems dated November 14*
(464) By the Koshi sea,
On the frozen Nozomi beach,
   Tasty seaweed grows.
I have long missed it by me,
Mourning it from day to day.

   If you are lucky,
And from the Nozomi beach
   Get any seaweed,
Share it with me, my friend.
I do not mind waiting long.

   Many years ago,
You and I picked together
   By the Koshi sea
The most delicious seaweed.
I have since remembered it.

257.   I have tried it on,
(480) And found it soothingly cool,
   My gracious donor,
This airy hemp summer gown
You, your devoted self, dyed.

258.   Many times I heard
(492) The ancients had treasured it,
   This majestic flask,
Now my own prize most precious,
Brought here by divine fortune.

259.   From today onward
(486) I shall never let dust fall,
   But early and late
I shall watch you lovingly.
My flask, stay not an exile.

260.   Many times over
(490) I take it in my own hands,
          Put it down again,
     And observe it far and near,
     My big flask beyond compare.

261.   Like an evergreen,
(397) Youthful and healthy for life
          You wish me to be,
     And toasting, you drink to me
          Cups of merry wine,
          Cups of merry wine,
     And I gulp, too, till I'm full,
          Cups of merry wine.

262.   For warming a house,
(398) Freshly constructed,
       Freshly constructed,
       Cups of joyful wine
     I keep drinking till I'm full,
     Countless cups of joyful wine.

263.   In a merry group,
(407) Seated all night round a fire,
          We drank cloudy wine,
     Breaking and burning dry twigs.
     Ah the great, great joy of it!

264.   Amid frogs singing,
(410) We will pluck on the hillside
          Fresh yellow roses,
     And, floating them in our cups,
     Let us drink masses of toasts.

265.   On a peaceful day,
(413) Under the sky calm and bright,
          I fell wine-tipsy,
       And dreamed a marvellous dream,
       Beneath cherry trees blooming.

266.   Coming to my house,
(227) Will you rest your noble eyes
       On my broad-leaved bashō tree?
         A cold wind rising,
       I have no means to guard them,
       Broad leaves of my bashō tree.

267.   Be you so inclined,
(245) Come and witness at my home
         How in plum bushes
       Spring warblers hop giddily,
       Spraying blossoms all about.

268.   This halcyon day,
(253) Treading on the silver snow,
         Come and visit me.
       Seated at my brushwood home,
       Let's gossip the night away.

269.   Again and again
(258) Fishermen dive for seaweed
         By the Maze beach.
       Come likewise oft visiting.
       I shall be waiting for you.

270.   With beloved you,
(260) I sit face to face all day,
       Talking quietly.
    If I must quit my life now,
    I leave no regrets behind.

271.   It is sweet of you
(264) To visit me this peaceful day;
       With pinks about you,
    Step by step up the hillside
    Plodding in the autumn breeze.

272.   High on a foothill,
(283) Beneath an age-old pine tree,
       At its sturdy base,
    We passed many friendly cups.
    That day we can never forget.

273.   My beloved friend,
(294) For you, none other but you,
       Under gray heaven,
    I went out between the rains,
    To gather fresh spicy greens,
       These.

274.   At Mount Kugami,
(296) Many steps up its steep side,
       In a shady field,
    I grew this big white radish.
    Eat your fill, I entreat you.

275.   In the shady grove
(303) Outside my pine-built cottage,
    Rain began to fall, drizzling.

       My beloved friend,
You must stay here in my house
A while longer till it clears.

276.   Stay a while longer.
(304)   The full moon will rise in time.
          Guided by its light,
    Why not walk home quite secure?
    A few strides will take you there.

277.   Stay a while longer.
(305)   The full moon will rise in time,
          Dispersing darkness.
    Along your way through the hill,
    Sharp chestnut burrs lie in wait.

278.   Between May showers,
(327)   Out of the clouds hanging low,
          I have just arrived.
    They will call me for certain
    A sutra-chanting spring bird.

279.   Amid autumn grass,
(331)   Feeding on the last glories,
          Flower to flower,
    I came to your cottage gate,
    Half-dreaming along the way.

280.   Bird as I may seem,
(338)   Shoot me not with a slingshot.
          Into your orchard
    I have slipped over the fence
    But to peck some wild berries.

281.   Up on the alcove,
(343) Sunny maple branches in a vase;
        Here at the desk,
    Unrolling maple-blazoned paper,
    Let us write poems, you and I,
        In praise of maple,
    And seated in this quiet home
    Glut ourselves with late autumn.

282.   Crickets all about,
(355) Autumn flowers still in bloom,
        At this shady hut,
    Let me stay and wait a while
    Till the moon rises, supreme.

283.   Adrift as a cloud,
(364) I have nought to hold me back,
        For I am a priest.
    With my heart void of desires,
    I must leave all to the winds.

284.   On a vernal hill,
(380) Cherry blooms above our heads,
        We play together,
    Each in accord with the rest.
    Let the long day have no end.

285.   Within a garden,
(384) Under the green willow trees,
        In a merry group,
    We dance and enjoy ourselves.
    Let such days come many times.

286. In a merry group,
(388) Let's sit on the grassy bank
   Outside my doorway,
  And watch together all night
  The perfect moon in the sky.

287. You all sing to me.
(389) I will in turn dance for you.
   In the sky above,
  With the clearest moon shining,
  How can we stay in our beds?

288. My beloved friend,
(421) You and I had a sweet talk,
   Long ago, one autumn night.
   Renewing itself,
  The year has rumbled along,
  That night still in memory.

To Yūshi in a dream

289.
(434) By what dreamy way
  Have you reached me, I wonder,
   On this icy night,
  When all the surrounding tops
  Hide themselves in frosty snow.

290. In a loud quarrel,
(441) I chid her in bitter words,
   But after a while
  I started to miss her much,
  And longed again to see her.

291.   No worldly lovers
(444) Have steadfast faces to show,
        So it seems to me,
    As each time they fall in love
    They must speak, not hide it.

292.   Let silvery snow
(225) Heap pile on pile upon earth.
    Should it cease to come down,
        My beloved friend,
    Would you perchance visit me,
    Climbing up the mountain road?

293.   At a holy shrine,
(527) Halfway up its steep slope,
    I stand and gaze all alone
        In astonishment
    At the heap of chaste snow,
    Fresh upon the sacred oaks.

294.   Amid remote hills,
(528) Down on sedge stubs withering,
        Snow everlasting,
        Snow everlasting,
    Comes in silence from the sky,
    Scarce seeming to stay so long,
        Snow everlasting,
        Snow everlasting.

295.   In soft spongy snow,
(539) Wrapped entire in its fullness,
        Stands the universe,
    And within its boundless space,
    Soft spongy snow keeps falling.

296.   Only a few days
(525)   Since calendar spring began,
              And yet already
         Frozen icicles by the eaves
         Thaw and melt away in drops.

297.   Glorious moon above,
(543)   Let me this peaceful evening
              Pluck at my pleasure
         Plum blooms to adorn my hair,
         This peaceful spring evening.

298.   Beyond the hedgerow,
(558)   Beating its wings in the yard,
              A cock crows loudly,
         Thinking himself just as sweet
         Perhaps, as the spring warbler.

299.   Outside my cottage,
(564)   Perched in the grassy footpath
              Between the paddies,
         A wagtail strains her windpipe,
         Now that spring has come again.

300.   Purple violets
(566)   Blooming all over the field,
              To a joyful lark
         I bend my ears all day long,
         Yet I have not had my fill.

301.   Over many hills,
(567)   Along a green mountain road,
              I plodded alone,
         When all at once by a brake
         A pheasant sent forth a cry.

302.   Of its own accord,
(569) My heart is enlarged with joy,
         Upon a spring day,
   While I sit and watch at ease
   A flock of songbirds at play.

303.   All across heaven,
(570) Ample as snowflakes flying
         Before a tempest,
   Comes down in a white shower
   A shroud of cherry blossoms.

304.   On Mount Kugami,
(587) In Koshi, my sweet homeland,
         I sit all alone,
   Feeling spring in the rustle
   Of evening air in my sleeves.

305.   By a stroke of luck,
(605) In the peach blossom season,
         At its very peak,
   I watch here at this village
   A stream aflame with blossoms.

306.   In a lonely place,
(608) A darksome hill on one side
         And a moon above,
   I scan far off in dim light
   Snowy blossoms of wild pear.

307.   Purple violets
(621) In my broken begging bowl
         And dandelions
   Put together for contrast,
   I say prayers unto Buddha.

308.   Amid woody hills,
(626) In a detached field high up,
       A bevy of girls
       Are busy transplanting rice,
       Their songs flying far away.

309.   Many hills around,
(633) In a mountain field high up,
       I see an old man,
       Bent beneath his water pail,
       Walk back and forth all day.

310.   Not for a moment
(642) Can I find peace for myself.
       Wherever I stay,
       I am of late forced to hear
       Cruel tales about the flood.

311.   At my shady house,
(647) My two legs stretched lazily,
       I find endless joy
       In hearing the summer frogs,
       Singing in a hillside field.

312.   Proudly imposing,
(1274) The Nozumi hill soars high.
       Today at my whim,
       I hiked over its tall ridge,
       And saw before me,
       Hung up like the white linen
       Women wash and dry,
       A sheet of deutzia blossoms
       In glorious bloom,
       While my ears were astounded
       By summer cuckoos,

Their season now come again,
Singing loudly in the woods.

 Ravished totally
By summer cuckoos singing,
 Fondly a-dreaming
Till darkness came over me,
I stood alone in the woods.

313. Hilltop to hilltop
(670) They must have followed along,
   The summer cuckoos
Singing shrill upon the trees,
Fluttering their wings in joy.

314. A short interval
(678) Between the wet rains of May
   Enticed me away.
Walking to the green paddies,
I found a cool wind sweeping.

315. Beyond and across
(684) The towering bamboo groves
   Beside my cottage,
A wind came swelling along,
Whispering soft to my ears.

316. The Weaver in love
(686) Must be standing on the bank,
   Tonight in Heaven,
Prepared, as the legend says,
To receive her dear Herdsman.

317.   Rosy underskirts
(689)   Flying in the autumn breeze,
            Tonight in Heaven,
        The Weaver must be waiting,
        The Starry Stream before her.

318.   Asleep, I fancy,
(692)   Awake, I probe with my eyes
            The divine Weaver
        And what she might be doing
        With her lover, love-making.

319.   Proudly imposing,
(704)   A mountain looms in the west.
        On its crest how much I wish
            A barrier gate,
        That I might arrest the moon,
        While it glitters in the sky.

320.   On an open ground,
(708)   Some steps up Mount Kugami,
            I watch all alone
        The moon rise above the pines;
        The whole scene ablaze at once.

321.   By my grassy house,
(711)   Brushing its low, humble roofs,
            Stands a bashō tree.
        The moon rests upon its leaves,
        Now the night is well advanced.

322.   Everyone fancies
(715) He has gone out of the world,
           Much as I do now,
       Watching the moon glittering
       Supreme in the cloudless sky.

323.   As the wind rises,
(718) Dewdrops come glimmering down,
           And pliant pampas
       Soon divide themselves to let
       The moon nestle there a while.

324.   In days old as gods,
(730) When concord long forsaken now
           Held the world over,
       There lived an ape, and a hare,
           And a fox besides,
       All bound in honest friendship.
           Awake at sunrise
       They played on hills and moors,
           And in the evening
       Side by side they lay sleeping.
           Thus for many years
       They lived together as friends,
           Till high in heaven
       The sovereign heard their fame,
           And wished to behold
       What he had heard others say
           In his own person.
       Thus, disguised as an old man,
           Feeble and sickly,
       He came stumbling towards them
           And demanded thus,
       "If my old ears can still hear,
           Differing in kinds,
       You live united in your hearts
           As one merry band.

Still, if you want to back up
  The name you enjoy,
Then raise me out of my slough
  And heal my hunger."
So saying, the old man dropped,
  Releasing his cane.
Anon the three went their ways,
  But after a while,
The ape returned from the hill
  Rising high behind,
Healthy chestnuts in his hands.
  He was soon followed
By the fox who came with haste
  From the stream before,
Some live catches in his mouth,
  All for the old man.
Now the hare alone leaped about
  Flying everywhere,
But when he at last came home
  Nothing in his hands,
The old man denounced him hard
  For his ill nature,
His lack of truth in his heart.
  In his deep remorse
The hare soon contrived a plan,
  And said to the ape,
"Will you climb the hill again
  To get some branches?"
And to the fox, "Can you build
  A bonfire for me?"
The two obeyed as true friends
  Should in such cases.
Then, into the flame, the hare
  Threw himself, alas,
Making for the strange old man
  A great sacrifice.
As soon as the old man learned
  The hare's loyalty,

His heart choked for deep pity,
   He cast up his eyes
Straight towards sacred heaven,
   And weeping aloud
He flung himself on the ground.
   After some moments
The old man struck his breast,
   And said to himself,
"I now perceive the loyal three
   Are equally true,
All trusty friends in sad need,
   And yet among them,
It was the good hare that made
   The best sacrifice."
So saying, the old man brought
   The corpse of the hare
To the bright hall of the moon
   And buried it there.
This, as I have heard men tell
   Through generations,
Is why on the cloudless front
   Of the shiny moon,
We have a hare placed in glory,
   And each time I hear
This tale so well known to me,
   I cannot help soaking
In the warm tears from my eyes
The sleeves of my sacred gown.

   Mortal as he was,
Once a hare offered himself
   Before an old man.
How my soul pines after him,
Hearing his tale once again.

   One mid-autumn night,
Watching the bright moon above,
   Of its own accord
My heart turns to the old tale
I have learned time after time.

        True as a mirror,
    A humble heart taught itself
        A great sacrifice.
    That heart must be commended
    Through countless generations.

325.   After long waiting,
(736) When a pine-cricket begins,
         How moving it is
     To hear a bell-cricket sing
         As if in answer,
     Waving its wings in the grass,
     Alas, wet with autumn dew.

326.   I have long waited,
(752) But at last it must have come,
         Mild autumn weather,
     For high on the mountainside,
     Cool-voiced dusk-cicadas sing.

327.   My grassy cottage
(765) Is at the back of your house,
         Among dewy fields.
     Each evening by the hedgerow,
     An endless choir of crickets.

328.   On this grassy hill,
(768) Bush-clovers and pampas blooms
         Let me snatch at will.
     I, for one, care not a straw
     If my holy robes are stained.

329.   Buried as if lost,
(777)   So that I must look for it,
            This deserted way,
        Covered up by bush-clovers,
        None else on it but myself.

330.   Over autumn hills
(779)   I have come my distant way,
            And of a sudden,
        Tall lacy flowers greet me,
        Waving in the morning dew.

331.   In an autumn gale,
(788)   Pliant pampas grass waves so,
            That I mistake it
        For breakers along the beach,
        Sweeping in the evening dark.

332.   Just for my solace
(801)   I have walked out of my home,
            Yet for the flowers
        Lush in the autumn grassland,
        Somehow I have lost my heart.

333.   In the autumn field,
(804)   Treading on the leaves of grass,
            A young girl walks by herself,
            Whoe'er she may be.
        Her bright scarlet underskirts,
        Can she ever keep them dry?

334.   On the autumn moor,
(807)   Glowing with the setting sun,
            Amid late flowers

Let me stay with butterflies,
Rapt in a dream of one night.

335.   Going and coming,
(814) I watch, each time admiring,
       Never satisfied,
The shiny dewdrops clinging
To pampas leaves by my gate.

336.   Dark melancholy
(832) Invades my heart in autumn,
       When I sit alone,
Hearing a cold shower pour
Down upon rustling bamboos.

337.   At my grassy house,
(220) You promised to view with me
       Red autumn maples.
I have therefore long waited
    For you to appear,
Standing up or else reclined,
    Always impatient.
Yet you have not come to me.
    Every day at dawn,
Frost lies thicker and thicker,
    And every evening,
Rain falls colder and colder,
    And often enough,
A chilly wind comes blasting,
    So that I much fear
The maple leaves will perish,
    And once blown away
They are gone past retrieving.
    Of lasting maples,
Stable in their scarlet hues,
    Durable in forms,

I have never heard them tell,
   Either in annals
From the age of ancient gods,
   Or in rustic tales
Passed on through generations,
   Or in Chinese books
For learned scholars to read.
   Thus wondering deep
While hourly waiting for you,
   Led to my wit's end,
I could not help cutting off
These maple twigs by my gate.

   By my grassy gate,
I have yet some maple leaves
   In their summer hue,
Still waiting for your visit,
In spite of the chilly frost.

   In the frosty dew,
Deep-dyed in glowing colours,
   Maples dazzled me.
I was forced to cut them off,
Fretting and longing for you.

338.   If my sacred gown
(833) Had sleeves truly big enough,
       I would surely spread it out
          Over the hillside,
       To shelter beneath its shade
       Red maple leaves on the hill.

339.   All green everywhere
(840) They appeared to me in spring,
         Early budding leaves.
       Now, matured by the autumn sun,
       Not one looks the same in hue.

340.   This autumn morning,
(841)   Hidden in the gathering mist,
            Maple leaves alone
        Can be descried now and then,
        Here at this mountain temple.

341.   Across and beyond
(842)   The tall mountains of autumn,
            I have come along,
        Flush maple leaves around me,
        So bright as to light my way.

342.   Careless is the dew
(849)   That gathers on autumn leaves.
            How careful they are,
        The leaves diversely coloured,
        Each in keeping with its kind.

343.   Distant or nearby,
(856)   Rid of all the maple leaves,
            Lofty ridges rise,
        The dim, open sky spreading
        High above, void of all joy.

344.   Amid forest trees
(861)   There on the hill opposite,
            A little stag stands alone,
            Late in October,
        While heaven weeps fitfully,
        Wet in the drizzling shower.

345.   In lowering dark,
(868)   Some steps up Mount Kugami,
           All of a sudden
        I heard a stag on the ridge
        Belling sweetly to its mate.

346.   Late in October,
(879)   When frosty showers drizzle
           Yesterday, today,
        For many days without cease,
           Outside my cottage,
        Battering down maple leaves
           In such profusion
        That every walk by my house
           Is deeply buried,
        Nightly seated by the hearth,
           A kettle boiling,
        I rip and burn dry branches
           In sheer solitude,
        While on the ridge opposite
           A wandering stag
        Bells longingly to its mate
           In icy darkness.
        No doubt I know well enough
           From my yesterdays
        That life is merely a dream,
           And yet in no way
        Can I give ease to my heart
           In this sad season.
        Over my matting, therefore,
           I spread my clothes,
        And lie down upon the floor,
           When an icy wind
        Directly from mountain tops,
           Comes attacking me
        Through many holes everywhere.
           Then I wrap myself

With all the robes in my house,
    And with my face hid,
Trembling and tossing about,
    I stay in my bed
In the dark of a cold night,
My eyes perfectly sleepless.

    One night in autumn,
The loud cascade by my house
    Is silenced at last.
Perhaps, on the mountaintops,
Snow has piled in heavy banks.

347.   Over and across
(1270) The slopes of Mount Kugami,
    I have come along
At twilight in late autumn.
    Down in the valley
Maple leaves are scattering,
    And on the ridges
Sad stags are heard belling.
    I am just as sad,
Yet I do not raise my voice;
    I watch in silence
Red maple leaves scattering,
My heart full of melancholy.

348.   Frosty autumn wind,
(884) Blow but gently, if you will,
    At my grassy house.
Here, it is lonesome enough
Without the din of the wind.

349.   Amid frosty hills,
(893) In a mountain field high up,
      A handful of ducks
    Is heard to cry in the dark,
    Now autumn has run its race.

350.   Lifted high above,
(910) Some steps up Mount Kugami,
      I live by myself,
    Confined by midwinter snow
      Falling every day
    Over the hills and valleys.
      Not a single bird
    Sings aloud about my house,
      And every footway
    For villagers to stride on
      Is deeply buried.
    Thus in complete seclusion,
      Behind a fast gate,
    My soul entirely consigned
      To the cataract
    Running down the icy slope,
      Endless as a rope
    Made by deft hands in Hida,
      Every day, for days,
    Each year, as long as I am,
    I live here confined alone.

      Now it seems to me
    High on the mountain ridges
      Icy snow has come,
    For the stream upon its way
    Has ceased its daily murmur.

351.   On my begging trip,
(925) I have not seen the village
      For many days now.

Today, as through yesterday,
Snow fell ceaselessly on me.

352.   How many more days
(933) Must I bide before springtide?
         Time and time again,
       Numbering the days and months,
       I look out for the fresh spring.

353.   No matter how loath,
(934) I must perforce say goodbye
         To the going year.
       How is it my thoughts alone
       Stay, unlike everything else?

354.   Seeing men quarrel
(937) On the last day of the year
         Like sworn enemies,
       I find them more depressing
       Than at any time year round.

355.   What reason you had,
(939) When you ran away from home,
         Like your holy gown
       Keep it ever in your heart
       Deep-dyed in the sacred hue.

356.   Amid frosty hills
(942) Stands all alone a scarecrow,
         As if cast away.
       Even he is thought to shield
       The bird gleaning beside him.

357.   Seeing others slip,
(945) Think that you must also err,
          And do not cavil.
       If you wish to know yourself,
       Use them as your looking glass.

358.   Yellow roses blow
(952) In single or double blooms.
          Double the double
       A hundred times, if you will,
       Still the single is singular.

359.   In the morning dew,
(955) Rising clear above the pond,
          Lotus flowers blow.
       Likewise, unspotted by dust,
       True worthies rise innocent.

360.   Solemn, I was told,
(957) Some stood on the holy ground,
          And I often took
       Them to be such as I heard of.
       Tested, none withstood my eye.

361.   Many years ago
(960) I fell to a lightless path
          Wholly unawares,
       When I saw a moon go down,
       Bright in the Akata hills.

362.   Not for a moment
(964) Can I find ease in my heart,
          Seeing everywhere
       Men engaged in mortal feuds,
       Causing a worldwide discord.

363.   By the riverside,
(970) Standing alone late at night,
           Did I then expect
       To see the glowing full moon
       Just behind the weeds adrift?

364.   Let it be adored,
(973) The loud bell from the temple.
           Once it awoke me
       From the vainglorious dream
       Of the world I had relished.

365.   Amid wooded hills,
(975) Hard beside a mountain field,
           I have my cottage,
       And from morning till sunset
           I beg for my food,
       Door to door, in the village;
           And in the evening,
       Soon as air starts quivering,
           My door firmly shut
       Against the frosty hill-wind
           Sweeping all about,
       I stay by the crackling fire,
           And muse by myself
       On the past long lapsed away.
       The world then seems a dream.

366.   Brood upon the past.
(976) The past is but a short dream,
           Gone in a twinkling.
       The present is yet more frail,
       More dreamlike in its brevity.

367.   Like cicada shells,
(984) This world is hollow inside.
      Real it might seem,
But it is empty throughout.
      This is the reason
I wrapped myself in a gown,
      And shedding away
My hair from my naked head,
      For days in a row,
Like a cloud floating above,
      I have roved along,
Without breaking my journey,
      And like a river,
Homeless, in all my roamings.
      Often at a shrine,
More often in a straw house,
      I slept by myself,
About human rights and wrongs
      Caring not at all,
My heart wholly surrendered.
      Yet it is a marvel
      Puzzling to myself
That I have torments within,
      Far too depressing
To be quenched by other men,
      And so ponderous
That I cannot turn them out,
      Nor in any speech
Can I state them well enough.
      The deepest abyss
Beside the plunging seashore,
      And the lofty hill
With its commanding summits,
      Will be in due time
Flattened to a level ground.
      My torments alone,
Do what I can to slake them,
Remain unchanged and rooted
Within the core of my heart.

Far away from men,
My gate shut with a wood bar,
I live all alone,
Yet somehow, within my heart,
Sore torments are gnawing me.

368.   Of the hollow world
(987) I have heard some men complain,
And priest as I am,
More alive than trees or rocks,
I feel my heart sore oppressed.

369.   Now that I am hurt
(989) By the anguish of the world,
Away in the hills,
I would presently lie down,
Like a dead tree or a stone.

370.   Since antiquity
(1006) It has always remained there,
Where I behold it.
Yet few have marched along it,
This covered walk before me.

371.   Pheasants cry aloud
(1009) Beside this ancient footpath
On a burnt moorland.
Who will now follow the wise
Who travelled here long ago?

372.   Icy winter streams
(1011) Frozen stiff down to their beds
Will finally thaw.
Yet, the hearts of mortal men
Stay fast-frozen all the time.

373.   Like honest bamboos
(1023) The virtuous stand straight up,
            In spite of the world
         Where deceitful tricks flourish
         And ill winds humble our heads.

374.   Like a water weed
(1028) I drift along here and there,
            Driven by the tide,
         So that I don't care a straw
         If you all call me bad names.

375.   One midwinter night,
(1033) Wrapped in a thin hempen gown,
            Shivering and tense,
         I wondered what I could spare
         To help people in their needs.

376.   Living all alone,
(1040) I do not fly from the world,
            Yet somehow I am
         Much more suited, by nature,
         To seek pleasure by myself.

377.   Like the rivulet
(1041) Running down in a trickle
            In a deep forest,
         I live here in quiet peace,
         Hidden away from the world.

378.   Seated in a shade,
(1045) I watch silver clouds arise
            And bury hilltops.
         What other gate have I here
         To bar me against the world?

379.　　*To a blank white fan*
(1052)　Searching in earnest
　　　Whether deep in my own heart
　　　　I have a selfish will,
　　　I find my heart wholly blank,
　　　Nothing but air blowing there.

380.　　No more apt emblem
(1056)　The world has to show itself
　　　　Than the weak echo
　　　That expires, as soon as born,
　　　With not a trace left behind.

381.　　*On my begging round, I went to*
(1062)　*Makiyama on February tenth.*
　　　　Standing in the field where once
　　　　stood the house of my friend,
　　　　Arinori, and seeing plum blossoms scattering,
　　　　I was reminded of the bygone days

　　　Once upon a time,
　　　Seated beneath a plum branch
　　　　We drank together,
　　　Sweet petals in our winecups.
　　　Now they lie useless on earth.

382.　　My hair glorified
(1067)　With a spray of budding plum,
　　　　I mused all alone
　　　On the past long gone before,
　　　How dear you were once to me.

383.　　Upon Twilight Hill,
(1086)　There is an ageless pine tree.
　　　　If it had a voice,
　　　I would no doubt hear from it
　　　All that it has known before.

384.   Wholly unawares
(1090) I was thrown to the bottom
              Of abysmal tears,
        Seated, facing an old book,
        Reading about bygone days.

385.   The running rivers
(1091) Can be checked by making dams.
              The towering hills
        Will be made flat by digging
              Little by little.
        Yet days and months, if gone,
              Are beyond recall.
        None of the marvellous books
              Witness otherwise,
        Nor have I heard a man speak
              Contrary to this.
        It must have been so, I think,
              Always in the past,
        While doubtless it is so now,
              And so it shall be
        For numberless years to come.
              Then of all evils
        The worst that can fall to us
        Is no other than creeping age.

              How obligingly
        They come seeking after me.
              Hidden far away,
        Deep inside a grassy house,
        I can not escape the years.

386.   Within the garden
(1104) A plum tree is in full bloom,
              Unmindful of me,
        Who spend in resigned silence
        The last hours of my journey.

387.   Have I, really,
(1107) Any friend who will help me
            To forget my age?
        I wondered alone, the night
        I left my cane by mistake.

388.   Had I been aware
(1111) That the years were after me,
            Upon the highway
        I would have put a fast gate
        To lock them away from here.

389.   So many reports
(1119) Of the Land of Lasting Joy
            Have edified me,
        Yet never can I get there,
        Not knowing the road to go.

390.   A tale too sacred
(1124) To tell with my own tongue,
            A legend too true
        To relate in mortal speech:
            Once upon a time,
        A sovereign in high heaven
            Detected at night
        A silver hair on his head,
            And early at dawn
        Called a minister of state,
            And directed him
        To fetch a pair of clippers
            Glowing in silver,
        And to cut his silver hair
            And put it within
        A big chest of silver sheen,
            And the sovereign

At his death ceded the gift
  To his successor,
And he in turn at his death
  Left it as a boon.
Thus, always from son to son,
  Endlessly in line,
I heard it was handed down,
The silver hair above price.

  Respect it in awe,
The silver hair on your head.
  Divine in its birth,
It has deigned to honour you
In your extreme advanced age.

  Do not despise it.
It could well come a herald
  From the underworld,
To call you out to darkness,
The silver hair on your head.

  Not for a moment
Hold it in worldly contempt.
  Now if not before
Learn to adore in your heart
The silver hair on your head.

  Of all the riches
That I can find in the world
  Nothing can equal
In price, no matter how dear,
The silver hair on your head.

391. Every winter night
(1129) Icy frost comes to the ground,
  And yet at sunrise
It melts, nowhere to be found.
  Each year in winter
Snow comes on us, piling up,
  Yet it thaws away

As spring sun begins to smile.
   Contrary to these,
The snow that covers our heads
   Grows the heavier
The more we advance in years.
   Renewing themselves,
Let the years run without end.
That snow shall never go away.

Newly fallen snow
Will melt away in due course.
   On the contrary,
The snow that ices our heads
Turns more silver every year.

392.
(1135)
Shortly after the death of Saichi

People come and go
On the village thoroughfare,
Numerous as sand on a beach,
   And yet among them
Not a young man looks, alas,
Like the one I knew so well.

393.
(1137)
Bright as a gilt bow
Spring had blown many flowers.
I went out to the fresh field
   To gather some greens,
Yet I could not fill my crate,
For no more were you with me.

394.
(1142)
To Mitsue, after his death, with a wreath

Once upon a time,
Seated on a rough straw mat,
   Together with you,
I watched the autumnal moon
Glowing all night in heaven.

395.
(1144)
As a boy, I used to have a close friend.
He left his home, and went to live
in Azuma. We remained out of touch
for many years, till I heard of his death

    Had I known it thus,
  I would have sent you my word
      Through a traveller
  Who went his way towards you
  Years before it grew too late.

396.
(1152)
When the village was hit by the plague

    Somehow forgetting
  It was the way of the world,
      I found it awesome
  To see countless people die,
  Fast as the leaves blown away.

397.
(1154)
    Hoping against hope
  For the deceased soul's return,
      I tarried all night,
  My cottage door left wide-open,
  Watching the bright moon above.

398.
(1168)
    Before or after
  Hardly matters in my view.
      Sooner or later
  We must abandon the world
  Hollow like cicada shells.

399.
(1188)
For the parents who are to commemorate
the first anniversary of
the death of their baby

    Just one year ago
  We snapped off to amuse you
      A tiny plum spray.
  This year, we break another
  To decorate your gravestone.

400.   I stood and I sat
(1192) In my vain attempt to bring
             Quiet to myself,
         And yet like the sea-tangle,
         My soul sank in a deep mire.

401.   In Koshi, my land,
(1218) At the marsh called Mishima,
             Many have told me,
         Birds float asleep together
         Their wings united in peace.

To see the five shadows truly as such
is the first step toward blissful peace

402.
(1231)   This world is empty,
         Dreamlike in its transience.
             Endless it may seem,
         Like a pheasant's downy tail,
             Trailing for ever;
         Yet look beneath the surface,
             For a hundred years,
         Or else, for a thousand years,
             Over the long past,
         And the route of our descent
             Slowly uncovered,
         We shall find it forking off
             At every junction
         So that we can never trace
             Our true ancestry.
         Thus standing up, we see not
             What is to be done,
         Nor can we rest well, seated.
             Like a cast-off gown,
         Our thoughts run in a tangle,
             Or like clouds above
         Our minds drift in heaviness
             And, too astonished,

We can neither talk nor move,
    But as ducklings do
On the boundless sea, we wail,
    Or as stray birds do,
We rack our throats for ever
    With sighs unending.
Yet I search within my heart
    A way out of this.
As a boat anchored in a port
    Embarks on its way
Over the deepest ocean waves,
Directly her cables are released
And all her hawsers rent asunder,
    Unbridled like air;
    Or as lofty grasses
    Rising in the shade
Under the spreading branches,
    Cut by huge sickles
    Or by sharp scythes,
    Are swept off apace:
    So in a like manner,
If we get rid at one stroke
    Of the five shadows
That make us this empty world,
    Seeing them as such,
Then without the least worry,
    Nothing to prick us,
We will surely live at ease,
Here on earth, until our end.

    Empty as we are,
How hard it is to perceive
    Our own vacuity.
Void is all we need to know
Of flesh, hearts alone holy.

    In the land of Tsu,
No matter how they may bloom
    At blithe Naniwa,
Alter not therefore your way,
But proceed to your own goal.

403.   Asked by anyone
(1236) If Ryōkan will leave behind
            A farewell poem,
        Tell him one word of prayer
        Will suffice me at my death.

404.   Numbers on water,
(1255) A wind will blow them away
            All in a moment.
        Much sooner it will vanish,
        Our own daring self-conceit.

405.   In Koshi, my land,
(1303) At the beach called Kakuda
            Many young ladies,
        Every day at dawn,
        Cheering each other, carry,
            Or at sunset, heat,
        Ocean brine to obtain salt.
            This is surely why
        The name of this uphill way
            Has for ever been
        Salt Hill Road and no other.
            It runs to the sky,
        Looking down a steep valley.
            Here horses falter,
        Threatened by its precipice.
            Even clouds linger,
        Not able to pass its height.
            This road, however,
        Has been flattened recently
            To a marked degree.
        Who had the marvellous skill
            To do such a feat,
        Whether he came from heaven,
            Sent down by a god
        To assist poor men on earth,
            Or he came to us

A helper from Buddha's land,
　　Or if his feat is
Just a twinkling of a dream,
　　Or a fact lasting,
I rejoice too much to know.
　　At a complete loss
What to say or what to do,
　　Watching all alone
The Salt Hill Road remedied,
I propose prayers of thanks.

　　No longer bitter
In its breathtaking ascent,
　　As in former days,
The Salt Hill Road remedied.
Our debt we must not forget.

406.　　*At Teradomari*
(1305)　On a temple ground,
　　On a temple ground,
In front of its stately hall,
　　Lofty trees aspire,
For how long no one can tell,
　　Lasting in respect,
God-like in their sturdiness.
　　In a humble house
Beneath these reverent trees,
　　I seek my shelter,
And each morning and evening
　　I come out walking
Here where giant trees tower,
　　And for many hours
I watch, never feeling tired,
These lofty trees above time.

　　As raging billows
Break against a rocky beach
　　Again and again,
So countless times visiting,
I admire the ageless trees.

407.   At Kugami,
(1314) There rises before a temple
   A lofty pine tree.
   Its upper branches
Cast a deep shadow beneath.
   Its middle region
Embraces the nests of birds,
   And its lower arms
Rub the tiles of the temple.
   Whether in winter
Deadly frost may fall on it,
   Or in late autumn
Tempests may come attacking,
   It stands unshaken.
Since the days of holy gods,
   So much respected,
This old pine without a peer,
Heaven-high on Mount Kugami.

408.   At Iwamuro,
(1315) Quite alone in a rice-field
   Exists an ancient pine tree.
   This rainy morning,
Soaked in the heavy drizzle,
It stands as if cast away,
   And left to itself,
If it were like us, I trust,
It would surely need a hood
And a warm raincoat as well,
My forsaken pine tree, alas.

409.   Far out in the sea,
(1328) The high hills of Sado loom
   Thin as an eyebrow,
   And near me, the evening sun
Glitters upon the spring sea.

410.   Within my garden
(1336) I grew autumn bush-clovers,
    Along with pampas,
Pansies, golden dandelions,
    A tiny silk-tree,
A plantain, morning glories,
    Hemp agrimonies,
An aster, moist dayflowers,
    And forget-me-nots,
And early and late each day,
    Never neglecting,
I fed them with clear water,
Defending them from the sun,
Doing what I could for them.
    By common consent
My good plants were exalted
    Above the others,
And I believed so too myself,
    Yet destiny desired
That one evening in mid-May,
    Or more precisely
At dusk on the twenty-fifth,
    Came a huge tempest,
Assaulting my garden plants
    With mighty anger,
Pulling them down with fury;
    And without pity
Poured upon them heavy rain.
    And all my flowers
Were ruined, torn to pieces.
    For days thereafter
My heart sank in depression,
    Yet no help I found,
For it was useless to blame
The wind above our reproach.

My garden flowers
I planted and nursed myself
  With genuine love,
I must learn to resign them
To the pleasure of the wind.

411.
(1344)

*To Arinori
on the last day of the year*

Close to Nosumi,
There was an ancient temple,
  And in its garden
A beautiful plum tree stood.
  It was your design,
Branches and roots together,
  To steal it away.
So one quiet spring evening,
  Over rocky hills,
Scaling slowly step by step,
  By a secret road
You came to the temple hall.
  That moment, alas,
Villagers spied your design,
  Rang the holy bell,
Beat the drums as if in war,
  And fell upon you,
All about the mountain side,
  In one noisy rout.
Ever since this fatal night,
  As a flower thief
You have won lasting renown,
  Wherever you went.
Nonetheless, as time passes,
  People grow weary
Of all they hear and behold.
  Perhaps, nowadays,
Left alone in perfect peace,
  At your grassy hut,

Twisting endless times over
　Your prodigal beard,
You may be musing all night
　At the dead end of the year.

412.　　　Bending my fingers,
(1352) I count time and time again
　　　The days gone away
Since my husband was buried.
　Today, I find out
Eight years I have expended
　In sheer solitude,
Slaving in a blighted house.
　Woman though I am,
Finding no comfort nor ease,
　Working like a man,
I have gained nothing, alas,
　But sad afflictions
Which day after day gnaw me,
　Till like a shadow
I look lifeless in my glass.
　Thus I am informed
Of the downright hollowness
　Of the empty world,
And of my flesh dead, alive,
　In its sinful doom.
Endless times day after day
　I seek speedy death
In my helpless wretchedness,
　Each time prevented
By the intense love I bear
　Toward my children,
　So that at a loss
What to speak or what to do,
　Just hiding myself,
I rack my throat in wailing
Early and late without rest.

A glass in my hand
I spent the whole day again,
　Watching all alone
The shade reflected therein,
The pale face staring at me.
　Nothing whatever
Is more helpless than I am,
I have lately come to know,
And grow on that very score
The more dismally helpless.

413.
(1356)

*In reply to Okura's poem
against living in seclusion*

Mortal beyond help,
Our hearts stay at variance.
　On that very score,
Each in his foolish fashion,
　Proud of his glory,
Puts forward his principles
　In books so legion,
None can ever read them all.
　More so than others,
In the goodness of my heart
　Or in verbal skill,
I am weak, and am therefore
　Averse to preaching.
Yet what everyone must know
　I must speak aloud
That no one may swerve away,
　And that is to say,
　Your ageing parents,
Your wife and many children,
　All your relatives,
You must completely forsake,
　And pious of heart,
Early and late without rest,
　You must meditate.

  That, and no other,
I believe, is the right way.
  Yet upon the earth
Few have force enough to do
  As they truly must.
Therefore, to encourage them,
  Or to entice them,
Leaders have said otherwise
  In different books.
  By a lucky chance,
You happened to peruse once
  A book of this kind,
And held it self-sufficient,
  Complete in itself.
Now I charge you to tell me
  With clean honesty
If you plead innocent still,
My well-read scholar, Okura.

Dewdrops on a Lotus Leaf
Poems exchanged between Ryōkan and Teishin

On hearing about my master's ball-bouncing

   This and no other
Seems to me the rightful way.
   You walk along it,
Gleefully bouncing your ball,
This endless road before you.

My master's reply

   Try it, if you will,
One two three four up to ten,
   And again it starts.
You, too, can march along it,
This endless road before you.

On seeing my master for the first time

   Having met you thus
For the first time in my life,
   I still cannot help
Thinking it but a sweet dream
Lasting yet in my dark heart.

My master's reply

   In the dreamy world,
Dreaming, we talk about dreams.
   Thus we seldom know
Which is, and is not, dreaming.
Let us, then, dream as we must.

*Late at night after a long conversation,
my master wrote*

   On our sacred sleeves
Dew has gathered thick and cold.
   On this autumn night,
The full moon reigns high above,
Matchless, in the cloudless sky.

I wished to stay longer by his side

   Face to face with you
I would sit for countless days
   And for endless years,
Silent like the cloudless moon
I admire with you this night.

My master's reply

   Changeless if you are,
Steadfast in your sacred faith;
   Long as a creeper,
Endlessly, for days and months,
We shall sit down side by side.

Poems exchanged at my leave-taking

   No doubt, I will come,
Since you kindly cheer me thus,
   If I have nought else
But the rank grass by the road
To guide me through my journey.

   Do as you have vowed,
And come to my thatched cottage,
   If it does please you,
Searching your way step by step
Through pampas leaves dew-laden.

My master sent me the following poem after some days

   Have you forgotten,
Or the road lost all too soon?
   For many days now,
Though I have waited each day,
You have not come to my place.

I sent the following two poems as my reply

   By worldly affairs
Bound within a certain house,
   Itself in the grass,
My feet and heart in discord,
I have not been free to come.

   In the sky above
The moon is glittering bright
   As if to guide me,
But near the hilltops beneath
Gloomy clouds still linger on.

*I was not at my own house
when I wrote these poems.
My master's reply*

   Out of their own will
Many have sacrificed themselves
   To their pious cause.
What makes you persist so long
In your dark life at the house?

   The glittering moon
Is bright enough to shed light
   Upon all the world
Reaching its farthest corners
And clearing the darkest minds,
Shining these days as of old
Alike on truth and falsehood.

   Yet unless you rise
Clear above those misty clouds
   About mountain-tops,
How can you, my dearest friend,
Hope to see the brightest moon?

I sent my reply as soon as spring came

   Without my plotting
Winter gloom has spent itself,
   And now, of itself,
Sunny spring weather has come
To where I stay long confined.

   Myself and others,
The false as well as the true,
   Without difference,
Receive equal light, when lit
By the bright moon in the sky.

   My heart awakened,
I find neither light nor dark
   Complete in itself,
For the soft moon lightens up
The whole of my dreamlike way.

My master wrote when I at last met him

   Nothing in the world,
Whether gold or silver pearls,
   Can be more of worth
Than this long-promised visit
From you, early in the spring.

   In the divine law,
There is nothing to stop you
   Doing what you like;
So long as you do all things,
Knowing them all as they are.

My reply

   Warmed by sunny air,
Frosty snow on mountain-tops
   Has started to thaw,
Yet the river stays mournful
Down in the rock-held valley.

My master's reply

    If on mountain-tops
Snow has started to dissolve,
    It will not be long
Before the stream on its bed
Begins to flow in good cheer.

My reply

    Flowers are silent
When asked about the wherefrom
    Of spring revival,
Yet, when they bloom in the sun,
No songbirds will stay behind.

    If untaught by you,
One hundred times one hundred
    I would have counted,
Not learning the simple truth
ten times ten is one hundred.

My master's reply

    I would stop, alas,
Bouncing balls by the roadway,
    If I knew the truth
Ten times ten is one hundred.
How can you hope to learn it?

We exchanged the following poems later at night

    Seated side by side
In front of our First Teacher
    Upon Mount Ryōzen,
We vowed our pledge together.
Let us keep it though we die.

Seated side by side
In front of our First Teacher
   Upon Mount Ryōzen,
We vowed our pledge together.
I will keep it though I die.

*Lecturing on the art of rhyming,
my master said*

   Not for a moment
Must you think our voices die
   Leaving no traces;
Truly more than what they are,
Words are equal to our hearts.

I bid farewell with the following poem

   I must set off now,
Wishing you health and quiet.
   I shall come again
As soon as cuckoos come back
singing loudly from the south.

My master's reply

   As a homeless man
I must drift on like seaweed.
   I am at a loss
As to where I should meet you
In summer, when cuckoos come.

   Come and visit me
In autumn, when on the moors
   Bush-clovers flower.
If you find me still healthy,
Let us deck ourselves bravely.

I visited him, however,
earlier than he told me to come

   Ever on the watch
For bush-clovers on the moor,
   Getting impatient,
Stamping on the summer grass,
I sought you at your cottage.

My master's reply

   It was kind of you
To visit me through the grass,
   Wet with summer dew,
Fretting far too much to wait
For the bush-clovers to bloom.

One summer, I visited my master's house
in his absence to find a fragrant
lotus flower in his vase

   I missed you today,
Coming to your vacant house,
   Yet in your absence,
I found the whole house alive
With the sweet smell of lotus.

My master's reply

   A white lotus spray
Fragrant still in a small vase
   Is all I can spare.
Think of me, each time you see
The sweet flower so arranged.

*One day, a friend of mine informed me
of my master's unexpected visit to Yoita.
I went there at once to meet him,
but he was ready to depart the next day.
During our conversation, it was suggested
that we should all call him "crow,"
for he was black not only in his robes
but also in the colour of his skin.
My master welcomed the suggestion
and, laughing, he wrote*

>   As free as a bird,
> I will roam across the hills
>   During my journey,
> Now that you all have agreed
> "Crow" is to be my nickname.

I replied at once

>   When a father crow
> Sets out from his forest home,
>   Aiming for a town,
> Will he e'er leave behind him
> His soft-feathered baby crow?

My master's reply

>   I'm not unprepared
> To carry out your sweet wish,
>   But what can you do,
> If someone, watching us both,
> Should surmise we are sinners?

My own reply

>   A kite is a kite.
> Sparrows are indeed sparrows.
>   Herons are herons.
> Should a crow walk with a crow,
> Who will take them for sinners?

At the sunset, however, I retired to my inn

   My sacred master,
Good night, till I come again
   Seeking after you.
Resting here at this cottage,
May you enjoy sleep and peace.

On the following morning,
however, my master came to my inn
at break of day; I welcomed him

   In writing poems,
In beating our bouncy balls,
   In picking flowers,
I will at once yield myself
Wholeheartedly to your wish.

My master's reply

   In writing poems,
In beating our bouncy balls,
   In picking flowers,
I shall use my hours and days,
Doubts still lingering in me.

My master promised to visit me
at my house in autumn, but his sickness
confined him to his cottage

   Every bush-clover
Has already passed its prime
   Upon autumn moors.
Yet prevented by ill-health,
I can not keep my promise.

*Instead of recovering, my master's health
deteriorated, and in winter, he was
so ill that, according to my friend,
he barred his door against any visitor;
I tried to console him with a letter*

   In your lonely bed,
Ease yourself a while longer.
   At your time of life,
What means it to you, master,
This brief dream of an illness.

*In reply, my master sent me the following poem,
unaccompanied by any other words*

   Come at once to me,
As soon as spring is with us.
   Here at my cottage,
I long to meet you once more,
Though for a twinkle of time.

*At the end of the year, my friend wrote to me
that my master had suddenly fallen
into a critical condition. Shocked, I went
to him in haste, but I found him seated
on his bed in a state of relative ease.
He welcomed me*

   Every day and hour
I have been waiting for you.
   Now that I see you
Seated at peace near my side,
I have nothing else to crave.

   Not unlike the dews
Fading fast behind the grass
   Of Musashino,
We all can stay in the world
No more than a passing dream.

*I decided to stay with him, and nurse him
in his sickness, but he grew weaker and weaker,
and it was obvious even to me that
he had only a few more days to live*

   To life or to death
I should cast a cloudless eye,
   Faithful to our vow.
Yet at this last leave-taking,
How can I restrain my tears?

*By way of reply, my master recited to me
the following lines in a low voice*

   Maple leaves scatter
At one moment gleaming bright,
   Darkened at the next.

*These lines were not of his own making,
but he liked them well enough to repeat them
from time to time. My master died on
the sixth of January in the second year
of Tenpō at the age of seventy-four.*

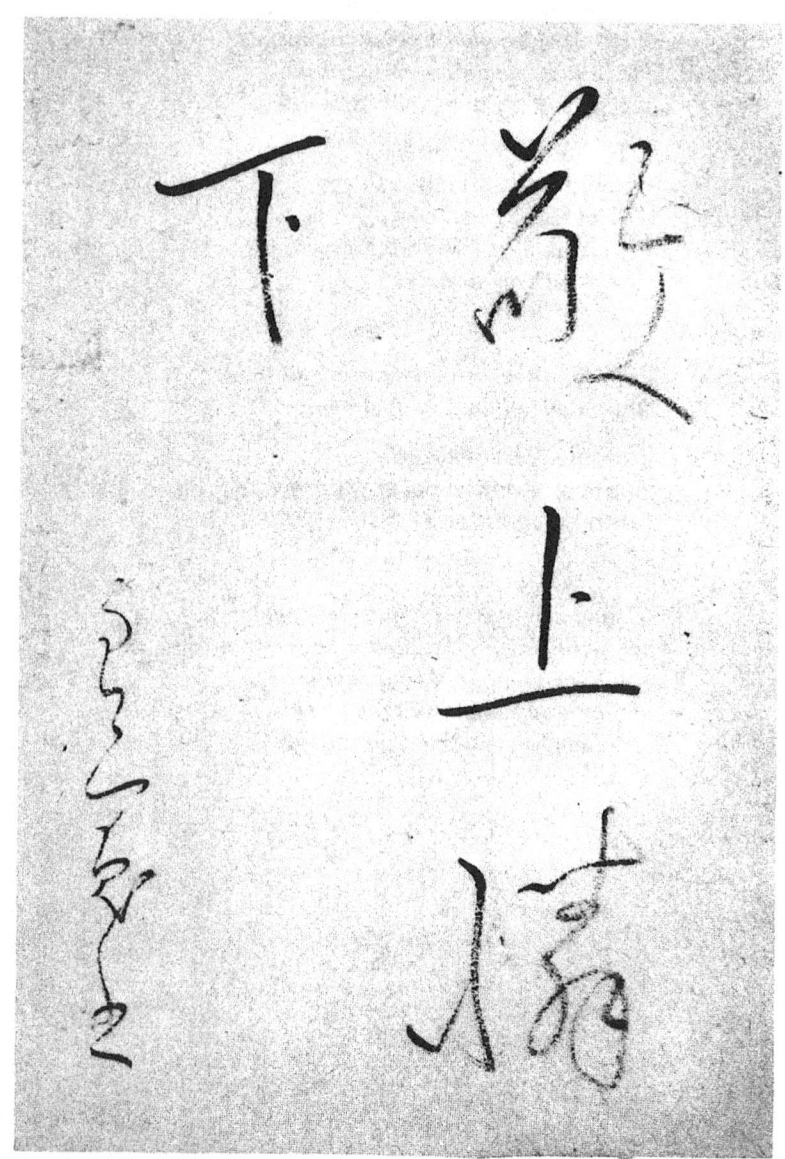

9. Confucian maxim in Ryōkan's handwriting:
Respect your seniors, and love your juniors.

EXPLANATORY NOTES

The numbers refer to the poems, except in the last note, where the parenthetical number refers to the page.

3. The grass-fighting game is a popular children's game in which a child entwines his blade of grass with that of his opponent, and by pulling hard, decides whose grass is the stronger.
7. The west is a holy direction, because Buddhism travelled eastward from India through China to Japan.
8. The bashō tree is a kind of banana tree, rather rare in Japan and loved by many poets. "The Prince of Pure Eating" is Buddha himself, and "the Beggar of Beggars" is his disciple, Mahākāśyapa. "Equal in eating, equal under the divine law we must be" was the teaching of Vimalakīrti.
16. Ryōkan's cottage was called Gogōan, which literally means "five bowls of rice." "Except for the gong" is an echo of a similar expression in *The Commentary of Tso (Tso Chuan)*. It is effective here because it emphasizes the emptiness of Ryōkan's cottage.
32. "A guest with spiked ears" is a reference to Bodhidharma, because he is so called in one of the Zen texts (*Hekiganroku* 55).
38. It must be borne in mind that when Ryōkan was granted permission to establish himself as a priest, his teacher gave him a certificate and a stick of mountain wood.
39. See the note to Poem 7 for the implication of "the western sky."
44. The fifth line is an echo of Bashō, who said in a poem written shortly before his death that his dreams kept revolving round the moors.
47. "The infinite He" refers to Buddha.
51. Buddha preached at Ryōzen (Gṛdhrakūṭa), a mountain in Bihar, and Hui-nêng taught at Sōkei (Ts'ao-hsi) in Kwangtung Province.
55. "Tō." is an abbreviation for Saitō, and probably refers to a friend of Ryōkan's who had a villa outside the city of Shibata.
57. "Great Sorrow" is a translation of Daihikaku, the name of a building that belongs to the Kokujōji temple. "Dragon's Well" is a translation of Ryūōsui, the name of a well located at the foot of Mt. Kugami.
58. The poem is about Gogōan.

63. The poem is a reply to Harada Jakusai, and is believed to be written in the same metrical scheme as his poem.
67. The seventh line contains a reference to Hsü Yu, who is said to have washed his ears when he was invited by the Emperor to serve him.
72. "The white rays" is an echo of Chuang-tzu (*Man in the World* 7).
73. The purple lawn is purely imaginary. It was believed to grow in ice-bound regions and provide food for hermits.
80. The first line is a reference to the Entsūji temple.
92. Both "the First Teacher" and "who preached at Mt. Ryōzen" refer to Buddha. "The great man who sorted out problems" is Nāgārjuna, "the wise teacher" is Bodhidharma, and "the man who rose by himself above the rest" is Dōgen, the founder of the Sōtō sect in Japan.
94. It has not been established what temples Ryōkan had in mind when he spoke of the three head temples. According to some commentators, they are the Ryūonji temple in Saitama prefecture, the Daichūji temple in Tochigi prefecture, and the Sōneiji temple in Chiba prefecture.
95. "The Five Mystical Stages" and "the Eight Blissful Methods" are subtle doctrines preached in the Tendai sect. The first of these refers to the different stages of Buddha's preaching career, and consists of *kegonji* (37 days), *agonji* (12 years), *hōdōji* (8 years), *hannyaji* (22 years), and *hokkenehanji* (8 years). The second refers to the different methods of salvation, and consists of *tonkyō* (instantaneous salvation), *zenkyō* (gradual salvation), *himitsukyō* (secretive salvation), *futeikyō* (unlimited salvation), *zōkyō* (salvation through the understanding of karma), *tsūgyō* (salvation through the understanding of the void), *bekkyō* (salvation through the understanding of equality), and *engyō* (salvation through perfect understanding).
100. "The ten temptations" are *muzan* (cruelty), *muki* (shamelessness), *shitsu* (envy), *ken* (stinginess), *kai* (resentment), *min* (sleepiness), *tōkyo* (violence), *konchin* (despair), *fun* (anger), and *fuku* (dishonesty).
101. The first line contains a reference to Hsü Yu, as in Poem 67.
111. "The Great Man of the Plum Hill" is Fa-ch'ang, his nickname being derived from the fact that he lived on the Plum Hill (T'ai-mêi).
122. "The holy book written at the temple, Eihei" is probably *Shōbōgenzō* written by Dōgen.
123. "The three phases of time" are past, present, and future. "The three stages of life" are stages dominated respectively by desire, matter, and spirit.

EXPLANATORY NOTES

124. The poem refers to the earthquake of 1828, which caused great damage and took a heavy toll of human lives in the Ryōkan country.
135. The poem refers to the *Bon* festival held in summer. Ancestral spirits are believed to return to this world for a brief visit during the festival days.
137. "The Narrow Stream" is a translation of Kyōga, the name of a river known also as Sebagawa.
138. "The Capital City" is Edo, and "the holy temple in a province by the sea" is the Entsūji temple. "The three divisions of time" are past, present, and future, and "the six steps of our journey" consist of *jigoku* (the infernal region), *gaki* (the starving region), *chikushō* (the animal region), *shura* (the demonic region), *ningen* (the human region), and *tenjō* (the heavenly region).
140. Ugan's cottage was called Tanomoan.
142. "My holy teacher" refers to Genjō Haryō.
150. "The Saint of the West" is Buddha, and "the important day due six days later" is December 8, the day commemorating his achievement of Buddhahood.
155. The poem is a reply to Abe Sadayoshi. "The Tempestuous Window" is a translation of Ransō, the name of his cottage.
161. "The Cloud Promontory" is a translation of Unki, a poetic name for Izumozaki.
170. "The Eternal Bridge" is a translation of Mannenkyō, whose location remains unidentified. To "sacrifice my brows" means, I think, to spare no pains.
171. "The perfect hand" is a reference to the calligraphy of T'ao Hung-ching.
183. "The Fragrant Pavilion" is a translation of Kōshukaku, the name of a building at the Enzōji temple in Fukushima prefecture.
189. A similar story is told about Unai Otome in the *Man'yōshū*.
197. "The cordless harp" refers, I think, to the human heart.
199. The poem simply describes the visual characteristics of the four different disciples of Buddha.
203. "A breath in everlasting pines" is taken from a poem written by Kōchi Hōin shortly before his death.
208. "The loyal forty-seven" is a translation of *gishi*, the name of a group of *samurai* who took revenge for the death of their lord by killing his enemy in 1702. Condemned to death by the government, they became famous as the flower of chivalry. They are celebrated in the Kabuki play, *Chūshingura*.
209. The poem is about Yuri, the wife of Sakutarō, a carpenter in Izumozaki. Her monument can still be seen there today.

212. The untouchables were social outcasts, who were placed at the lowest level of society and often discriminated against by other people.
214. The sixth and seventh lines are based on *The Analects of Confucius (Lun-yü)*, IX, 2 and VII, 18.
218. The poem was written for Kimura Motoemon to decorate the roll of sutras he donated to the Ryūsenji temple.
220. The poem is not in Tōgō Toyoharu's *Ryōkan Kashū* which I have used as the basic text. I have taken it from Yoshino Hideo's *Ryōkan Shū*, Koten Nihon Bungaku Zenshū, 21, Chikuma Shobō, 1966.
223. Takano refers, I think, to Kōyasan, in which case, however, we should have "the land of Ki" instead of "Tsu."
225. The association of Waka no Ura with *waka* and its power of soothing the human heart like balm is at least as old as the *Shinkokinshū*, and its association with spring balm at least as old as Bashō.
239. The poem is to be found in a letter to Kera Shukumon.
243. The poem accompanies a portrait of Ryōkan by Henchō.
246. The poem was sent to Abe Sadayoshi, who wrote a reply.
251. The poem was sent to Teishin, who wrote a reply.
254. The poem was written by Ryōkan to thank his brother, Yūshi, for his gift. "My living breath" refers, I think, to the poem itself.
255. The poem is for Abe Sadayoshi.
261. The poem is for Abe Sadayoshi.
266. See note on Poem 8 for an explanation of the bashō tree.
268. The poem is for Suzuki Chinzō.
270. The poem was written by Ryōkan when he received a visit from his brother, Yūshi.
271. The poem is for the priest Daiki of the Tokushōji temple in Yoita.
274. The poem is for Abe Sadayoshi, who wrote a reply.
275. The poem is for Ōmura Mitsue, who recorded it in his account of his visit with Ryōkan.
276. 277. These two poems are for Abe Sadayoshi.
278. "A sutra-chanting bird" is a translation of *uguisu* (spring warbler), whose song resembles the name of the holy text called *Hokekyō* (*Saddharma Puṇḍarīka Sutra*).
281. The poem is for Abe Sadayoshi.
282. The poem was written by Ryōkan at Kyūkindō, the house of Yamasaki Rakusai.
283. The poem was written by Ryōkan when he was about to leave the house of Abe Sadayoshi.
286. The poem is for Harada Arinori.

290. The poem was sent to Oyoshi, a lady in the household of Yamada Tokō.
312. The poem was written by Ryōkan on April 20 on his way to Nozumi across Mt. Kugami.
316, 317, 318. These poems refer to Tanabata, the July 7th festival to celebrate the annual reunion of the Weaver and the Herdsman in the sky. The Weaver and the Herdsman are two stars (Vega and Altair) separated by the Milky Way, and traditionally they are believed to meet once a year on this festival day.
324. The story of this poem was taken from the *Konjaku Monogatari* V. 13.
344. The poem is to be found inscribed on Ryōkan's tomb in the Ryūsenji temple.
364. "The loud bell from the temple" is a translation of *Gionshōja no kane no koe*, and "the vainglorious dreams of the world" is a translation of *shogyō mujō no yume*. In both of these, Ryōkan is indebted to the opening passage of the *Heike Monogatari*.
374. The poem is a reply to Yūshi, who accused Ryōkan of acting lightheartedly like a prostitute.
376. The poem accompanies the only portrait of Ryōkan done by the poet himself.
383. "Twilight Hill" is a translation of *Yūgure no Oka*, a hill situated to the southeast of Mt. Kugami.
387. The poem was written by Ryōkan when he left his walking stick by mistake at the house of Hoshi Hikozaemon in Teradomari.
402. "The five shadows" is a translation of *goon*, and consists of *shiki* (body), *sō* (fancy), *ju* (sense), *gyō* (will), and *shiki* (reason).
405. "Salt Hill Road" is a translation of Shionorizaka, a steep mountain pass halfway between Yoita and Shimazaki.
407. The pine tree celebrated in this poem is dead now, but its huge trunk can still be seen at the Kokujōji temple.
410. The poem was written shortly after the typhoon of May 1830.
(216). "The First Teacher upon Mt. Ryōzen" refers to Buddha.

GLOSSARY OF PROPER NAMES

Personal names are in the usual Japanese and Chinese order (the family name followed by the given name). Place names are distinguished from personal names by the use of italics, and some place names are indicated on the Map of the Ryōkan Country, p. 4. The numbers and parenthetical numbers that follow the explanation refer respectively to the poems and pages in the present volume where the names are to be found.

Abe Sadayoshi (d. 1838): the village head of Watanabe, a disciple of Ōmura Mitsue; a friend and admirer of Ryōkan. He was known also as Teichin. His house was called Ransō. (49), (51), 155n, 246n, 255n, 261n, 274n, 283n

Akahito: see Yamabe no Akahito.

Akashi: a beach on the Inland Sea, near Kōbe. Together with Suma, particularly famed in Japanese literature for its beauty. 224

Akata: a group of hills to the west of Mt. Kugami. 361

Amaze: a town on the Japan Sea, situated next to Izumozaki. In Ryōkan's times, an important port for the Island of Sado. The rivalry between Amaze and Izumozaki caused the downfall of Ryōkan's family. The Kōshōji temple where Ryōkan took the tonsure is situated in this town. (30), (31), (36), (43)

Ame no Kagoyama no Mikoto: the god enshrined at the Yahiko shrine. Traditionally it is believed that, sent by the Emperor Jinmu, he taught the villagers how to net fish, how to make salt, and how to grow rice. (47)

Arimaro: see Kada no Arimaro.

Arinori: see Harada Arinori.

Ariwara no Motokata (d. 953): a poet of the *Kokinshū*, and a grandson of Ariwara no Narihira. Ingenuity and technical excellence characterize his poems. (11)

Ariwara no Narihira (825-880): a poet of the *Kokinshū*, representing, together with Ono no Komachi, the period of the so-called Six Poetic Geniuses (Rokkasen). Described as a passionate lover in the *Ise Monogatari*, and criticized by Ki no Tsurayuki as having too much heart and too few words. (11), (12)

Asama: an active volcano in Nagano prefecture, central Japan.

Asatsuna: see Ōe no Asatsuna.

Avalokiteśvara: a Bodhisattva, gifted with complete enlightenment and placed at the head of the merciful, whose permanent dwelling is in the blissful mountain called Potalaka. Identified in China with Kuan-yin, whose Japanese name is Kannon or Kanzeon. 112

Azuma: a name given to the eastern provinces of Japan, especially the district around Edo. 395

Bashō: *see* Matsuo Bashō.

Bodhidharma (470-543): an Indian priest, the founder of Zen in China. He is believed to have sat in meditation for nine years at the Shao-lin temple on Sung shan, a mountain in Honan province. Self-righting dolls in his image are popular in Japan under the name of Daruma. 32n, 92n, 205

Buddha (c. 563-c. 483 B.C.): Gautama Siddhārtha, the founder of Buddhism, whose parents were Śuddhodana (Pure Eating), King of the Śākyas, and Queen Māyā. After his happy youth he renounced the world and became an ascetic. After six years, however, he realized the futility of ascetic practice and, sitting in deep meditation under the shade of a bo tree, received complete enlightenment at the age of 35. Henceforth, he returned to the world he had renounced, and preached enlightenment. Ryōzen (Gṛdhrakūṭa), a mountain in Bihar, is famous as a place where he preached. 8n, 47n, 51n, 92n, 93, 141, 150n, 198, (216)n

Bundai: *see* Suzuki Chinzō.

Ch'ang-an: an ancient capital of China, which flourished under the Han and T'ang dynasties, its Japanese name being Chōan. 123

Chia Tao (777-841): a poet of the T'ang dynasty, famous for his great deliberation over the line, "A priest knocks at the gate beneath the moon." (23)

Chikage: *see* Kato Chikage.

Chikkyū: *see* Kaizu Kanpei.

Chiyō: *see* Ch'ih-yang

Ch'ih-yang: the place in Anhwei province where Nan-ch'üan taught his disciples. 201

Chōan: *see* Ch'ang-an

Chōmei: *see* Kamo no Chōmei.

Chuang-tzu (c.369-c.286 B.C.): a Chinese philosopher and interpreter of Taoist thought; known in Japan as Sōji. His theories of spiritual emancipation and all-embracing unity probably appealed to Ryōkan. (39), 72n

Confucius (c.551-c.479 B.C.): a Chinese philosopher, known in Japan as Kōshi. His theories of li (order) and jen (humanity) formed the foundation of political and educational thought in feudal Japan. Ryōkan read his *Analects* as a child. (33), 214

GLOSSARY OF PROPER NAMES

Daichūji: a temple in Tochigi prefecture, famous during the Tokugawa period. 94n

Daki (dates unknown): the head priest of the Tokushōji temple in Yoita. 271n

Daikoku: a Japanese god of prosperity, holding the hammer of luck in his hand and a big bag of wealth over his shoulder; often identified with Ōkuninushi no Mikoto. 204

Dainin (1781-1811): a priest born in Izumozaki, whom Ryōkan met in Kyōto; the compiler of the *Mugishū* in which he defended Ryōkan's poetry. (21), 145

Daiten (dates unknown): a priest in Kyōto, whom Ryōkan praised for having mastered the art of quiet breathing. 146

Daruma: *see* Bodhidharma.

Dōgen (1200-1253): the founder of the Sōtō sect in Japan, who studied Zen first under Eisai in Japan, and then under Ju-ching (Nyojō) in China. He prized sitting in deep meditation more than reading the sutras or saying prayers. Ryōkan read both his collection of holy writings called *Shōbōgenzō* and his collection of *waka* called *Sanshōdōei*. (12), (15), 92n, 122n

Ebisu: a Japanese god of luck, pictured as holding a fishing pole in his hand with a fish on its line; often identified with Hiruko, deformed son of Izanagi and Izanami. 204

Echigo: *see* Etsu.

Edo: the city which is now Tōkyō, the seat of the Tokugawa government. The Edo period (1603-1867) constitutes the late feudal age of Japan. (4), (5), (20), (30), (38), (42), 138n, 156

Eiheiji: the temple established by Dōgen in Fukui prefecture in 1246. 92, 122

Eizō: Ryōkan's name in his childhood. (32), 87

Emmadō: the small temple where Teishin retired after she took the tonsure, situated in the village of Fukushima near Nagaoka. (52)

Enchō: *see* Yamamoto Enchō.

Enmeiji: the temple of which Ryōkan's brother, Enchō, was the head priest; situated in Izumozaki. (34)

Enō: *see* Hui-nêng.

Entsūji: the temple where Ryōkan studied Zen under Kokusen, situated in Tamashima, Okayama prefecture. (36), (37), (40), 80n, 122, 138n, 172, 173, 174, 175

Enryō: *see* Yen-ling.

Etsu: the three provinces, Echizen, Etchū, and Echigo, are often grouped together as Etsu; but when Ryōkan says Etsu, he usually means Echigo where he was born. Koshi is synonymous with Etsu. (31), (39), (46), 133, 256, 304, 401, 405

Fa-ch'ang (752-839): a priest of the T'ang dynasty, a disciple of Ma-tsu. He is said to have solved the mystery of life, when he heard his master's words, "Each living heart is a Buddha in itself." He lived on the mountain called T'ai-mêi. His Japanese name is Hōjō. 111n

Fan K'uai (d. 189 B.C.): a Chinese general who assisted the First Emperor of Han to win many victories. He outwitted his enemy Hsiang Yü by a display of patience at Hung-mên. Illustration I

Fugan: *see* Nan-ch'üan.

Fugen: *see* Samantabhadra.

Fuji: the highest mountain in Japan, an active volcano in the days of the *Man'yō* poets. (7), (39)

Fujie (dates unknown): a physician defended by Ryōkan, probably a friend of Kera Shukumon. 151

Fujiwara no Hideyoshi (1184-1240): a poet of the *Shinkokinshū* who rose to be the governor of Dewa province, but after a defeat in battle became a monk under the name of Nyogan. His poetry, usually characterized by close observation of nature, was praised by the Emperor Gotoba. (11)

Fujiwara no Kiyotada (d. 958): a poet of the *Shinkokinshū*, son of Fujiwara no Kanesuke. His poetic style is often called plain. (11)

Fujiwara no Michinobu (972-994): a poet of the *Shinkokinshū* whose early death was deplored as the loss of a poetic talent in the *Konjaku Monogatari* and *Ōkagami*. (11)

Fujiwara no Shunzei (1114-1204): a poet of the *Shinkokinshū* and editor of the *Senzaishū*; known also as Toshinari. His poetry is rich in profound mystery (*yūgen*) and symbolic beauty (*en*). He is reported to have recited his poems in tears late at night, sitting under a dim light and bending over a fire pot. (12)

Fujiwara no Tameie (1198-1275): one of the editors of the *Zokukokinshū*, a son of Fujiwara no Teika. His poetic style is relatively plain. At his death, his three sons, Tameuji, Tamenori, and Tamesuke, quarrelled, and caused the splitting of the Fujiwara family into three separate houses, each representing a different school of poetry. (5)

Fujiwara no Teika (1162-1241): one of the editors of the *Shinkokinshū*, a son of Fujiwara no Shunzei; known also as Sadaie. His poetry is characterized by ethereal beauty (*yōenbi*), often involving an aura of magic and romance, although he leaned toward a more realistic style in his later years. He possessed a very complex nature, highly emotional and sympathetic but obstinate and intellectually aloof. (5), (12)

Fujiwara Seika (1561-1619): a Confucian scholar of the early Edo period, the founder of neo-Confucian studies (*jukyō*) in Japan. He was greatly influenced by Chu-tzu. (20)

Fujiya Mitsue (1768-1823): one of the *Man'yō* revivalists of the Edo period, also a Shintō theologian. His poetic theory is based on the concept of the living power of language (*kotodama*). (13)
Fukui: a village situated to the north of Mt. Yahiko. 228
Fukushima: a village near Nagaoka, where Teishin's temple, Emmadō, was situated. (52)
Ganjōji: a temple in the town of Hokkedō near Yoshida, where Keizan was the head priest. 164
Genjō Haryō (d. 1814): the head priest of the Kōshōji temple, in Amaze, who is believed to have given Ryōkan the tonsure; a disciple of Kokusen. (36), 142n
Genroku: a period of Japanese history, 1688-1703, marked by general prosperity and the rise of the merchant class. 208
Genzaemon (dates unknown): the man who proposed to build a new house for Ryōkan. His family name remains unknown. (51)
Ghoṣa (dates unknown): an Indian priest during the reign of King Kanishka; worshipped as a Bodhisattva under the name of Myō'on in Japan. 199
Gogōan: the cottage where Ryōkan lived from 1804 to 1816, situated on the west slope of Mt. Kugami, several hundred yards below the Kokujōji temple, to which it belongs. The cottage was originally built for Mangen about a hundred years before Ryōkan moved into it. The present building is a modern reconstruction and does not fit Ryōkan's description. The cottage derives its name (Five bowls of rice) from the fact that Mangen received five bowls of rice every day from the temple. (42), (44), (47), 16, 58n
Gōho: see Ho-p'u.
Gōmoto: a village on the coast of the Japan Sea, near Teradomari, where, according to Tachibana Konron, Ryōkan found a cottage to live in on his return to his native district. (41)
Gṛdhrakūṭa: a mountain in Bihar, India, where Buddha often preached, its Japanese name being Ryōzen, Ryōjusen, or Gijakusen (Gijjhakūṭa). 51n, 92, (216)
Gyōkei (d. 1165): a poet of the *Shinkokinshū*, son of the Emperor Shirakawa, a priest of the Onjōji temple in Shiga prefecture. (11)
Hachisuke (dates unknown): a beggar who lived under the bridge called Ryōgokubashi in Edo. After living a miserable life as an untouchable, he killed himself by jumping into the river. Ryōkan wrote a poem in sympathy. 212
Hakuba: see Po-ma.
Hakuga: see Po-ya.
Hakuyū (dates unknown): a hermit of the middle Edo period, who lived in seclusion in the mountains of Kyōto. 104

Han: a Chinese dynasty which lasted from 202 B.C. to 220 A.D. 129
Han Kai: *see* Fan K'uai.
Han-shan (dates unknown): a Chinese hermit of the T'ang dynasty, who, together with Shih-tê, lived in seclusion on Cold Mountain (Han shan) in the T'ien-t'ai range, Chekiang province. His Japanese name is Kanzan. Ryōkan had a copy of his poems and prized it better than a holy text. Among Chinese poets he had the greatest influence on Ryōkan. (23), (24), (25), (26), (27), (28), 25, 186, 215
Harada Arinori (1763-1827): a physician in the village of Nakajima, near Mt. Kugami; Ryōkan's classmate at Ōmori Shiyō's school; known also as Jakusai (or Shakusai) and celebrated by Ryōkan as a flower thief. (50), 63n, 154, 193, 286n, 381, 411
Hattori Nankaku (1683-1759): a scholar-poet of the Edo period, a disciple of Ogyū Sorai. His publication of Li P'an-lung's anthology of T'ang poetry was a great contribution to the development of *kanshi*. His poetry is characterized by beauty of diction and metrical precision. (20), (21)
Hayashi Hōkoku (1721-1773): a scholar of the Edo period, who became the head professor of Shōheikō in 1757. He wrote the inscription for the monument to Yuri, wife of Sakutarō. Ryōkan calls him Professor Rin. 209
Hayashi Razan (1583-1657): a Confucian scholar of the early Edo period, a disciple of Fujiwara Seika. Supported by Tokugawa Ieyasu, he built a private school at Ueno in Edo, which later became the official school of the Tokugawa government under the name of Shōheikō. (20)
Heian: the name given to the capital of Japan established in 794, now called Kyōto. The Heian period runs from 794 to c.1185. (18)
Henchō (d. 1876): Ryōkan's religious disciple, born in the town of Shimazaki. According to Teishin, he tried to compile an anthology of Ryōkan's Chinese poems. He left a portrait of Ryōkan. 243n
Henjō (816-890): a poet of the *Kokinshū*, a high-ranking priest, and founder of the Genkeiji temple near Ōtsu. His poetry was criticized by Ki no Tsurayuki as lacking sincerity (*makoto sukunashi*). (11)
Hida: a mountainous province in Central Japan, now part of Gifu prefecture. Ropes were a famous product of this region in Ryōkan's days. 350
Hideko: *see* Yamamoto Hideko.
Hikone: a city on the east coast of Lake Biwa, where Kokusen took the tonsure. (36)
Hitomaro: *see* Kakinomoto no Hitomaro.
Hokkedō: a town near Yoshida. The Ganjōji temple was situated nearby. 164

Ho'on: *see* P'ang-yün.
Ho-p'u: a district in Kwangtung province, once famous for the production of pearls, its Japanese name being Gōho or Gappo. 113
Hōsai: *see* Kameda Hōsai.
Hotei: *see* Pu-tai.
Ho-yang: a district in Honan province, its Japanese name being Kayō. Ryōkan probably had the etymological meaning (south of the river) in mind when he used the name of this district. 190
Hsin-fêng: a town in the suburbs of Ch'ang-an, famous for its fine rice wine. Its Japanese name is Shinpō. 188, 190
Hsü Yu (dates unknown): one of the earliest of legendary Chinese hermits. When he was invited by the Emperor Yao to serve him, he is said to have washed his ears, and when he was presented with a dry gourd by a friend as a substitute for a drinking vessel, he is said to have thrown it away as something unnecessary and cumbersome. His Japanese name is Kyoyū. (26), 67n, 101n
Huang T'ing-chien (1045-1105): a Chinese poet of the Sung dynasty; a disciple of Su Shih. He was popular in Japan among the Zen priests of the Muromachi period. (20)
Hui-k'o (487-593): The second Chinese Zen patriarch, the author of *Mumonkan (Wu-mên-kuan)*, his Japanese name being Eka (or sometimes Sōka). 172
Hui-nêng (638-713): The sixth Chinese Zen patriarch, who studied Zen under Hung-jên (Kōnin) but spent most of his life simply splitting firewood and pounding rice. He was nicknamed Beastly Blind. His rival Shên-hsiu (Jinshū), established a separate school, causing the splitting of Chinese Zen into the so-called North and South schools. Hui-nêng's Japanese name is Enō. 51n, 111, 173
Ichigyō (dates unknown): a priest who remains unidentified. 160
Iizuka Hisatoshi (dates unknown): one of the early biographers of Ryōkan, and author of *Tachibana Monogatari*. (35)
Ikei (d. 1822): a daughter of Miwa Nagataka; a nun who looked up to Ryōkan as a spiritual teacher. She took the tonsure after her husband's death. She was known also as the nun Ikyō. (51), 156
Ikkyū Sōjun (1394-1481): a Zen priest of the Muromachi period, head priest of the Daitokuji temple in Kyōto, and the author of the *Kyōunshū*, a collection of Chinese poems. His rebellious character is best expressed in his satirical poems. (19)
Inan: *see* Yamamoto Jirōzaemon Yasuo.
Inland Sea: a stretch of sea surrounded by Honshū, Shikoku, and Kyūshū; dotted with numerous small islands. (37)
Ise: a shrine situated in Mie prefecture; historically, the most important of all Shintō shrines in Japan. The inner shrine is dedicated to

Amaterasu Ōmikami, and the outer shrine to Toyouke Ōkami. During the Edo period, pilgrimages to this shrine became popular under the name of *Ise mairi*, because they were thought to bring prosperity and long life. 178, 226

Issa: *see* Kobayashi Issa.

Issairo (dates unknown): a physician in the village of Kugami. 162

Itoigawa: a city on the coast of the Japan Sea. Because of his illness, Ryōkan was forced to make a stop here on his way to his native country. The city is the birthplace of Sōma Gyofū, a Ryōkan scholar. The Gyofū museum contains some important Ryōkan materials. (40), 179

Iwamuro: a village at the foot of Mt. Yahiko. There was a huge pine tree standing all by itself in a rice-field near this village. 408

Iwa no Hime (dates unknown): according to the *Kojiki*, the consort of the Emperor Nintoku. She is one of the earliest of the poets of the *Man'yōshū*. Her poetry reveals her passionate nature, and legend has it that she was extremely jealous. (9)

Izumozaki: a town on the coast of the Japan Sea, where Ryōkan was born. His father, Inan, and his brother, Yūshi, both became the headman of this town in succession, but the rivalry between Izumozaki and the neighbouring town, Amaze, caused their downfall. In Ryōkan's days, the town was a port for the island of Sado. The Ryōkan museum erected in this town contains some valuable materials. (30), (33), (34), (36), (40), (42), 161n, 209

Izuruta: the name of a shrine in the town of Shimazaki. 21

Jakusai: *see* Harada Arinori.

Jien (1155-1225): a poet of the *Shinkokinshū*, a high-ranking priest, and author of *Gukanshō*, a history book. The Emperor Gotoba says that among the poems of Jien, those written in a relatively plain style are the best, and Fujiwara no Teika praised him equally with Saigyō. (12)

Jizen (dates unknown): a priest who remains unidentified. 159

Jittoku: *see* Shih-tê.

Jizōdō: a town on the west bank of the Sebagawa, one of the estuaries of the Shinano River, where Ryōkan's teacher, Ōmori Shiyō, opened his school. (32)

Jōdo Shinshū: *see* Shinran.

Jōgenji: a temple in Izumozaki, where Sone Chigen, the husband of Ryōkan's sister Mikako, was the head priest. (34)

Kada no Arimaro (1706-1751): a scholar-poet of the Edo period, the author of *Kokka Hachiron*, in which he upheld the style of the *Shinkokinshū*. When he left the service of Tayasu Munetake, who was a *Man'yō* revivalist, Arimaro recommended Kamo no Mabuchi as his successor. (13)

Kagawa Kageki (1768-1843): a scholar-poet of the Edo period, and author of *Niimanabi Iken*, in which he criticized Kamo no Mabuchi's artificial attempt to revive the *Man'yō* style. Kageki himself preferred the style of the *Kokinshū*. His followers formed a group called Keienha. (5), (6)

Kaizu Kanpei (dates unknown): Ryōkan's friend in the village of Takehana near Jizōdō; known also as Chikkyū. 148, 149

Kakinomoto no Hitomaro (fl. 680-700): a poet of the *Man'yōshū*; probably a courtier of low rank, who served in remote provinces, such as Iwami. His poetry, however, is marked by the nobility of its sentiments and the use of elevated poetic language. (8), (9), (10), (11)

Kakuda: a village on the coast of the Japan Sea, near Mt. Yahiko. In Ryōkan's days, salt was made on its sandy beach. 405

Kamakura: the city where Minamoto Yoritomo established a shogunate in 1185. The Kamakura period runs from 1185 to 1333, followed by the Muromachi period, 1333 to 1573. These periods were marked by the rise and prosperity of the *samurai* class. (19)

Kameda Hōsai (1752-1826): a Confucian scholar and poet of great fame in Edo; known also as Bōsai. Together with Yamamoto Hokuzan, he strongly attacked Ogyū Sorai and other imitators of T'ang poetry. Ordered to close his school in Edo in 1790 by the government, he went to Echigo and was welcomed by Ryōkan. (21), (46), 158

Kamo no Chomei (1155-1216): a poet of the *Shinkokinshū* and author of *Hōjōki* and *Mumyōshō*. The first of these is a collection of essays, and the second is a work of criticism in which he praised the poetic style that possessed a suggestive quality (*yojō*). (5)

Kamo no Mabuchi (1697-1769): a scholar-poet of the Edo period. Together with Tayasu Munetake whom he served as a retainer, he upheld the *Man'yō* style. His critical views are expressed in his *Kaikō*. He became a leading spirit in the literary world, and gathered many disciples. (5), (6), (7), (12), (13)

Kankakei: *see* Wan-hua-hsi.

Kannon: *see* Avalokiteśvara.

Kan Sazan (1748-1827): a scholar-poet of the Edo period, who taught Rai San'yō at his school in Fukuyama; known also as Chazan. (21)

Kanzan: *see* Han-shan.

Kaoru: *see* Yamamoto Kaoru.

Katami: *see* Ōtomo no Katami.

Katō Chikage (1735-1808): a scholar-poet of the Edo period, and disciple of Kamo no Mabuchi; the author of *Man'yōshū Ryakuge*, which Ryōkan borrowed and read. (6)

Katō Kyōtai (1732-1792): a *haikai* poet of the Edo period and friend of Yokoi Yayū and Yosa Buson. Ryōkan's father, Inan, was also a friend of his. Kyōtai visited Inan at Izumozaki in 1775. (31)

Katsura: the name of the river in the southwest of Kyōto where Ryōkan's father committed suicide. (40)

Kayō: *see* Ho-yang.

Keizan (dates unknown): the head priest of the Ganjōji temple in the town of Hokkedō. 164

Kera Shukumon (1765-1819): the village head of Maki ga Hana, near Jizōdō; a friend and supporter of Ryōkan. Ryōkan is said to have copied the *Saddharma Puṇḍarīka Sutra (Hokekyō)* for him. (49), 150, 239n

Kera Yoshishige (1810-1859): a son of Kera Shukumon, and one of the early biographers of Ryōkan; the author of *Ryōkan Zenji Kiwa*, which contains some important testimony about Ryōkan's poetic ideas. (6), (7), (50)

Ki: the name of the largest river in Ki province, now Wakayama prefecture. 135

Kikkatsu: *see* Hui-nêng. 111n

Kimura Motoemon (1776-1848): a rich farmer in Shimazaki; known also as Toshizō. Ryōkan spent his last years in the cottage attached to the house of Motoemon, and also wrote a letter of admonition to Motoemon's son, Shūzō. Motoemon's house is now a museum, containing the largest collection of Ryōkan's manuscripts. (51), (52), (53), (55)

Ki no Tsurayuki (868-945): a poet and one of the editors of the *Kokinshū*; the author of *Tosa Nikki*. He was a great promoter of the courtly style, and his poetry is marked by a delicate combination of wit and emotion, art and spontaneity. (11)

Kisen (dates unknown): a poet of the *Kokinshū*, and a legendary hermit, whose poetry was criticized by Ki no Tsurayuki as being somewhat hazy in its wording (*kotoba kasuka*). (11), (16), (17)

Kiyotada: *see* Fujiwara no Kiyotada.

Kobayashi Issa (1763-1827): a *haikai* poet of the late Edo period, whose poetry is marked by a bold use of vulgar terms and animal images; the author of *Ora ga Haru* (cf. the version by the present translator, entitled *The Year of My Life*). He commented on the cause of Ryōkan's father's suicide in *Kabuban*, attributing it to an attack of beriberi. (4), (40)

Kōchi Hōin (d. 1363): a priest of the Shingon sect, whose body is preserved at the Saiseiji temple in Nozumi, where Ryōkan lived for some time. 203

Kokan Shiren (1278-1346): a Zen priest of the Kamakura period, famous for the beauty of his prose and poetry. (19)

Kokujōji: the name of the temple on Mt. Kugami founded by Taichō in the Nara period. It belongs to the Shingon sect, and an interesting story about this temple is to be found in the *Konjoku Monogatari*. Gogōan, the cottage where Ryōkan lived for many years, belongs to this temple, which is still a beautiful place, surrounded by ancient trees. (44), 57n, 407n

Kokusen (d. 1791): a Zen priest of the Edo period, the abbot of the Entsūji temple in Tamashima, and Ryōkan's teacher. Genjō Haryō, who gave Ryōkan the tonsure, is also believed to have studied under Kokusen. Born in the province of Musashi, Kokusen took the tonsure at the Seiryōji temple in Hikone. (36), (37), (38), 38n, 165

Komachi: *see* Ono no Komachi.

Kondō Manjō (d. 1848): a poet of some fame in Edo, and a native of Tamashima, who says he met Ryōkan in Tosa on the island of Shikoku. (38)

Konkō: *see* K'un-kang.

Konron: *see* K'un-lun.

Koshi: *see* Etsu.

Kōshōji: the temple in Amaze where Ryōkan took the tonsure and studied Zen under Genjō Haryō before his removal to the Entsūji temple in Tamashima. (36)

Kōshukaku: a building belonging to the Enzōji temple in Yanaizu, Fukushima prefecture.

Kōyasan: a mountain in Wakayama prefecture where Kūkai built in 816 the Kongōbuji temple, the centre of the Shingon sect. Ryōkan went there to pray for his father's repose. (40), 135, 177, 223n

Kugami: the mountain on which the Kokujōji temple and Gogōan, the cottage where Ryōkan lived for more than ten years, are situated. The Otogo shrine is at its foot. Together with Mt. Yahiko, it is an outstanding landmark of the Ryōkan country. (44), (47), 32, 39, 57n, 138, 159, 230, 231, 233, 248, 274, 304, 312n, 320, 345, 347, 350, 407

Kuma no Mori: a village in the vicinity of Jizōdō. 163

K'un-kang: a group of mountains in west China, where precious stones were dug up; often identified with K'un-lun. 113

K'un-lun: a legendary mountain in west China, where it was believed that an earthly paradise existed. Its Japanese name is Konron. 196

Kyōga: an estuary of the Shinano river, known today as Saikawa. In

Ryōkan's days, it was also called Kyōsen or Sebagawa. Ōmori Shiyō's school was on its west bank, whence his pen name, Kyōsen. 137n, 138

Kyōtai: *see* Katō Kyōtai.

Kyōto: in Ryōkan's day, capital of Japan; seat of the Imperial Court from 1180 to 1869. Ryōkan's father committed suicide there. Kaoru, Ryōkan's brother, established his fame as a scholar at the court, and Ryōkan himself lived in and out of Kyōto for some time after his father's death. Ryōkan also met Dainin and Daiten here. (32), (34), (40), 135, 146, 178

Kyūkindō: *see* Yamasaki Rakusai.

Li Ho (790–816): a poet of the T'ang dynasty whose poetic career, showing early talent, was curtailed by his premature death. His poetry is marked by rich sensual beauty and morbid melancholy. His influence on Ryōkan is felt in two poems. (23)

Li P'an-lung (1514–1570): a poet of the Ming dynasty whose anthology of T'ang poetry was published in Japan by Hattori Nankaku, and has ever since exerted a great influence. (20)

Li Po (701–762): a poet of the T'ang dynasty, perhaps the most romantic of the poets of his day, in both the choice of his subject matter and its handling. He always wrote under the influence of alcohol, and is said to have drowned when he jumped into the Yangtze river to embrace the moon's reflection. Ryōkan wrote a poem in praise of him. (23), (24), (27), (51), 211

Liu Tsung-yüan (773–819): a poet of the T'ang dynasty who wrote beautiful nature poems while living in exile. Ryōkan is indebted to his poem entitled "River Snow." (24)

Li Yü (937–978): the last king of the Southern T'ang, who lived as a prisoner at the Sung capital and died in captivity. His early poems are lighthearted, but his later poems express a sense of futility and remorse. (23), (24)

Mabuchi: *see* Kamo no Mabuchi.

Mahākāśyapa (dates unknown): an Indian priest, who was praised as the best of the ten disciples of Buddha. When Buddha preached at Mt. Gṛdhrakūṭa, Mahākāśyapa is said to have understood his teacher's meaning better than anyone else. His Japanese name is Maka Kashō. 8n

Maitreya (dates unknown): an Indian priest of the fifth century, worshipped in Japan as a Bodhisattva under the name of Miroku. His return to this world in the very distant future is believed to bring universal salvation to mankind. 215

Maki ga Hana: a village near Jizōdō, where Kera Shukumon was the village head. (49)

Makiyama: a village near Mt. Kugami, where Harada Arinori was born. 381

Mangen (d. 1718): the guest priest of the Kokujōji temple for whom Gogōan, the cottage where Ryōkan later lived, was built. He was a friend of the head priest, Ryōchō, and helped him to restore the temple. (44)

Mañjuśrī (dates unknown): one of the ten disciples of Buddha, worshipped in Japan as a Bodhisattva under the name of Monju, venerated as a patron of wisdom, and often paired with another Bodhisattva called Samantabhadra (Fugen). 199

Mannenkyō: a bridge that remains unidentified. 170n

Manzei (fl. 704): a poet of the *Man'yōshū*, sent to Dazaifu as the head priest of the Tsukushi Kanzeonji temple; a friend of Ōtomo no Tabito. His poem (351) on the transience of the world became famous, and probably exerted an influence on Ryōkan. (9)

Matsudaira Sadanobu (1758-1829): a feudal lord of the Edo period who rose to power in 1787 when he was appointed chief of the Council of Elders. He reversed the liberal policy of Tanuma Okitsugu, and tightened government control on economic and cultural activities. (43)

Matsuo Bashō (1644-1694): a *haikai* poet of the Edo period, and the greatest exponent of this genre in its formative years. Born in Ueno, Iga province, he studied poetry under Kigin, and established himself as a *haikai* teacher in Edo. He travelled extensively, and in addition to *hokku* and *renga* (linked verse), left many travel sketches (see the present translator's version, entitled *The Narrow Road to the Deep North*). Ryōkan's father, Inan, was a distant disciple of his through Shikō and Hokumei. Ryōkan himself wrote a poem in praise of Bashō. (4), (26), (31), 44n, 207, 225n

Maze: a fishing village at the foot of Mt. Yahiko. 269

Michinobu: see Fujiwara no Michinobu.

Michizane: see Sugawara no Michizane.

Mikako: see Yamamoto Mikako.

Minamoto no Tsunenobu (1016-1097): a poet of the *Shinkokinshū* and a courtier of the late Heian period, also famous as a skilled musician. His poetry is often praised for the freshness of its natural descriptions. (12)

Miroku: see Maitreya.

Mishima: a village near Shimazaki, where there was a marshy pond. 401

Mitsue: *see* either Fujiya Mitsue or Ōmura Mitsue.
Mitsuzōin: a temple in Teradomari, where Ryōkan stayed for a short time. (42)
Miwa Gonpei (d. 1852): a rich merchant in Yoita from whom Ryōkan borrowed Chikage's commentary on the *Man'yōshū*. (51)
Miwa Saichi (d. 1807): a relation of Miwa Gonpei, and disciple of Ryōkan. His premature death was deeply mourned by Ryōkan. 141, 142, 143, 144
Monju: *see* Mañjuśrī.
Motokata: *see* Ariwara no Motokata.
Motoori Norinaga (1730-1801): a great scholar-poet of the Edo period, and disciple of Kamo no Mabuchi. Instead of *makoto* (sincerity) which his teacher stressed, Norinaga based his critical ideas on *mono no aware* (intense feelings aroused by the beauty of things). This difference induced him to choose the *Shinkokinshū* as a literary model. Among his works, *Isonokami Sazamegoto* and *Ashiwake Obune* are important as discussions of *waka*. (6), (13)
Murako: *see* Yamamoto Murako.
Muromachi: a period in Japanese history from 1333 to 1573, marked by continuous troubles under the uncertain rule of the Ashikaga Shogunate. (19)
Musashi: one of the eastern provinces of Japan, including within its boundaries what are now Tōkyō, Saitama, and Kanagawa. (36)
Musashino: a wide stretch of grassland in Musashi province. (222)
Myōgen: *see* Yamamoto Mikako.
Myōgo (dates unknown): Ryōkan's aunt on his mother's side. 135
Myō'on: *see* Ghoṣa.
Myōshin (dates unknown): Ryōkan's aunt on his mother's side. 135
Nagaoka: a city on the east bank of the Shinano river, where Teishin's father served as a retainer to his lord. (52)
Nāgārjuna (dates unknown): an Indian priest who contributed greatly to the development of Mahayana Buddhism, his Japanese name being Ryūju. 92n
Nan-ch'üan (748-834): a priest of the T'ang dynasty and disciple of Matsu. He lived at Ch'ih-yang in Anhwei province and taught many disciples. When two rivals fought for the possession of a cat, he is said to have cut it in two halves to show them the futility of quarrelling. His Japanese name is Nansen Fugan. 51, 201
Naniwa: a thriving city on the coast of the Inland Sea, now called Ōsaka. 402
Nankaku: *see* Hattori Nankaku.
Nansen: *see* Nan-Ch'üan.

Nara: an ancient capital of Japan, older than Kyōto. The Nara period is from 710 to 784. (18)
Narihira: *see* Ariwara no Narihira.
Niigata: a city on the coast of the Japan Sea, where Ryōkan visited his friend, the priest Ugan. (30), 139
Nisen (dates unknown): a priest who remains unidentified. 159
Norinaga: *see* Motoori Norinaga.
Notoya: the name of the house of Kimura Motoemon, indicating his connection with Noto province. (51)
Nozumi: a village on the coast of the Japan Sea, near Mt. Yahiko; known also as Nozomi. The Saiseiji temple where Ryōkan lived for a short time is situated here. (42), 256, 312, 411
Nukata no Ōkimi (fl. c.690): a poet of the *Man'yōshū*. She was loved by both the Emperor Tenmu, and the Emperor Tenji. Her poetry is marked by regal dignity and splendour. (9)
Ōe no Asatsuna (886-957): a poet of the *Wakanrōeishū*; a famous scholar-historian of the Heian period. (19), (24)
Ogyū Sorai (1666-1728): a famous scholar of the middle Edo period, known as the leader of the group of scholars called Kobunji Gakuha. He stressed the importance of linguistic analysis of ancient texts. He insisted that in *kanshi* the "Great Poets" of the T'ang dynasty should be used as models. (20)
Oka Kamon (dates unknown): the author of *Hokuetsu Yūjō*, in which he attributes the cause of Ryōkan's taking the tonsure to political disillusionment. (35)
Okumura Gohei (dates unknown): Teishin's father, who served as a retainer to the feudal lord of Nagaoka. (52)
Okura: *see* Yamanoue no Okura.
Ōmi: a province around Lake Biwa, now Shiga prefecture. 229
Ōmori Shiyō (d. 1791): a Confucian scholar who taught Ryōkan in his boyhood. Shiyō was trained in Edo and opened a school in Jizōdō, his native town, in 1770. The school was on the west bank of the Kyōsen, an estuary of the Shinano river, which gave him his pen name. He closed his school in 1777, and he went to live in Tsuruoka, Yamagata prefecture. Ryōkan wrote a poem at his grave. Ryōkan was also a close friend of Shiyō's son, Kyūko. (32), (33), 137
Ōmura Mitsue (1753-1816): a poet of the Edo period, and a disciple of Kamo no Mabuchi. He had among his disciples Abe Sadayoshi. He visited Ryōkan at his Gogōan in 1801, and left a short account of his visit. (7), (45), (49), 275n, 394
Ono no Komachi (dates unknown): a poet of the *Kokinshū*, representing, together with Ariwara no Narihira, the period of the so-called Six

Poetic Geniuses (Rokkasen). Ki no Tsurayuki says her poetry is "deeply touching, but very feminine." Her beauty in her youth and her misery in her later years have become a popular legend. (11)

Otogo: the name of the shrine dedicated to Takemorosumi no Mikoto, situated at the foot of Mt. Kugami. Ryōkan lived in a cottage attached to the shrine from 1816 to 1826. Otogo means literally "the youngest son." Takemorosumi no Mikoto was believed to be the youngest son of Ame no Kagoyama no Mikoto, to whom is dedicated a larger shrine at the foot of Mt. Yahiko. (47), (48), (51), 86, 233, 248

Ōtomo no Katami (fl. 772): a poet of the Man'yōshū and a contemporary of Ōtomo no Yakamochi. (8)

Ōtomo no Tabito (665-731): a poet of the Man'yōshū who lived in Kyūshū for three years as the Governor of Dazaifu. He was the father of Yakamochi and a friend of Yamanoue no Okura. His poetry is marked by an interest in Chinese literature and the melancholy of a disappointed courtier. (9)

Ōtomo no Yakamochi (716-785): a poet of the Man'yōshū, and one of its compilers. He was the first son of Tabito and, like his father, was sent to various places as a governor and general. In poetry also, he continued his father's interest in Chinese literature, but shows a greater leaning towards aestheticism. (10)

Oyoshi (dates unknown): a lady in the household of Yamada Tokō, whose role in the family remains unidentified. 290n

Ozawa Roan (1723-1801): a scholar-poet of the Edo period, who criticized the classicism of Kamo no Mabuchi. He was praised by Motoori Norinaga as the best poet in Kyōto. His critical views influenced Kagawa Kageki. (13)

P'ang-yün (dates unknown): a disciple of Ma-tsu. After a two-year stay with his teacher, he is said to have lived in isolation and to have supported himself by making bamboo baskets. His daughter, Ling-chao-nü, took them to a city and sold them. Ryōkan wrote a poem to praise her. Her Japanese name is Reishōjo, and her father's Japanese name is Hō'on or Hō Koji. 173, 202

Po Chü-i (772-846): a prolific poet of the T'ang dynasty who excelled in many different types of poetry. His political poems were ignored in Japan, but his poems dealing with his private experiences became popular among the Japanese, especially during the Heian period, perhaps because their language was thought to be natural and easy to understand. Po Chü-i was a leading inspiration to the poets of the Wakanrōeishū, and many Japanese poets imitated him in their attempt to combine wit and emotion. (18), (19), (20), (23), (24)

Po-ma: the name of the first Buddhist temple in China, situated near Lo-yang; its Japanese name being Hakuba. It is believed that two Indian priests, supported by the Emperor Ming of the Han dynasty, established it in 67. 92

Po-ya (dates unknown): a famous musician in the Ch'un-ch'iu period. He is said to have stopped playing his harp after the death of his beloved friend, Chung Tzu-ch'i, because no one else understood the beauty of his art. His Japanese name is Hakuga. 196

Pu-tai (d. 916): a priest of the late T'ang dynasty who always carried a big bag on his shoulder and went around begging. He is called Hotei in Japan, and often identified with Maitreya, or regarded as one of the seven gods of fortune. 200

Rai San'yō (1780-1832): a famous scholar-poet of the Edo period; the author of a popular history book, *Nihon Gaishi*. He also wrote *kanshi* in a relatively free, unaffected style. (4), (21)

Reishōjo: *see* P'ang-yün.

Rin: *see* Hayashi Hōkoku.

Roan: *see* Ozawa Roan.

Ryōgoku: a district in Edo, near the Sumida river, famous for firework displays and *sumō* wrestling during the Edo period. 212

Ryōzen: *see* Gṛdhrakūṭa.

Ryūonji: a temple in Saitama prefecture, famous during the Edo period. 94n

Ryūōsui: the name of the well located at the foot of Mt. Kugami. 57n

Ryūsenji: a temple in the town of Shimazaki, where Ryōkan's grave is located. (55), 344n

Sado: an island in the Japan Sea, about 30 miles away from Izumozaki, famous for its gold mines. Ryōkan's mother was born on this island. (30), (32), 222, 409

Saichi: *see* Miwa Saichi.

Saigyō (1118-1190): a poet of the *Shinkokinshū* and the author of the *Sankashū*. He was an imperial guard, but is said to have deserted his wife and children to become a monk. He spent most of his life as a wandering priest, thus becoming a model for later poets, including Bashō. His poetry is characterized by *sabi* (a sense of loneliness). (11), (12), (13), (15)

Saiseiji: a temple in the village of Nozumi, where the body of Kōchi Hōin, a priest of the 14th century, is preserved. Ryōkan lived here for a short time. (42)

Saito (dates unknown): a man who had a villa outside the city of Shibata, near Niigata, whose personal name remains unidentified. 55n

Sakanoue no Iratsume (dates unknown): a poet of the *Man'yōshū*; a half-sister to Ōtomo no Tabito and the consort of Prince Hozumi, and, later, the wife of her half brother, Ōtomo no Sukunamaro. Her poetry is marked by technical excellence and intellectual brilliance. (9)

Sakimaro: *see* Tanabe no Sakimaro.

Sakutarō (dates unknown): a carpenter in Izumozaki, whose wife, Yuri, became famous for her devotion to her mother-in-law. 209n

Samantabhadra: a Bodhisattva worshipped in Japan under the name of Fugen. As a patron of merciful action, he is often paired with Mañjuśrī, who is a patron saint of wisdom. 199

San'yō: *see* Rai San'yō.

Seiryōji: a temple in Hikone, Shiga prefecture, where Kokusen, Ryōkan's teacher, took the tonsure. (36)

Seki Chōun (dates unknown): the husband of Teishin, a physician in the village of Ryūkō near Ojiya. After his death, Teishin became a nun. (52)

Sekizaemon (dates unknown): a farmer who lived near the village of Kuma no Mori, whose family name remains unidentified; probably a friend of Ryōkan. 163

Senkei (dates unknown): a priest of the Entsūji temple whose duty was the humble one of growing vegetables and looking after kitchen requirements. Ryōkan was deeply impressed by his devotion and wrote a poem in his honour. (37), 165

Shakuan (dates unknown): a priest at the Entsūji temple, to whom Ryōkan complained about the prohibition of drinking enforced there after Kokusen's death. 175

Shakutai Kannon In: a temple which remains unidentified. 96

Shibata: a city near Niigata. A man named Saitō had a villa in its vicinity. 55n

Shichisei (dates unknown): a friend of Ryōkan's with whom he rode bamboo horses as a boy. He remains unidentified. 147

Shih Ching: the earliest anthology of Chinese poetry, containing court poems and popular songs. Its influence is felt in the *Man'yōshū*. (22)

Shih-tê (dates unknown): a Chinese legendary hermit who is believed to have lived with Han-shan in complete seclusion in the T'ien-t'ai mountains, Chekiang province. 215

Shikishima: an ancient name for Japan, used often as a pillow-word for Yamato, which also means Japan. 254

Shikoku: one of the four major islands of Japan, facing Honshū (the main island) across the Inland Sea. (38)

Shimazaki: the town where Ryōkan spent his last years, situated about six miles to the south of Mt. Kugami. Ryōkan's grave is here.

Kimura Motoemon's house is now a museum, containing the largest collection of Ryōkan's manuscripts. (51), (52), (55)

Shingon: a sect of Buddhism, established in Japan by Kūkai in the Heian period, its center being at Kōyasan. The sect derives its name from Mantra (True Word), and emphasizes the importance of rites and rituals. (44)

Shinpō: *see* Hsin-fêng.

Shinran (1173-1262): a priest of the Kamakura period, the founder of Jōdo Shinshū, a sect of Buddhism which emphasizes the importance of *nenbutsu* (reciting prayers to Buddha). Although the sect was persecuted at first, Shinran's influence spread among the lower classes. (52)

Shionorizaka: a steep mountain pass between Yoita and Shumazaki. 405n

Shiro: *see* Tzu-lu.

Shiyō: *see* Ōmori Shiyō.

Shōheikō: the official school of the Tokugawa government, originally established by Hayashi Razan as a private school. It enjoyed the highest prestige as a centre of Confucian studies. (20)

Shokushi Naishinō (d. 1201): a poet of the *Shinkokinshū*; known also as Shikishi Naishinō. She was a daughter of the Emperor Goshirakawa. Her poetry is meditative in tone and expresses deeply-felt love. (11)

Shūbi (dates unknown): a painter in Niigata who once visited Ryōkan at Gogōan. 157

Shukumon: *see* Kera Shukumon.

Shunzei: *see* Fujiwara no Shunzei.

Sōka: *see* Hui-k'o.

Sōkei: *see* Ts'ao-hsi.

Sōma Gyofū (1883-1950): a poet-critic of the Taishō and Shōwa period; one of the promoters of naturalism in Japan. He approached Ryōkan from a humanistic point of view. His books on Ryōkan exhibit his sympathy and understanding, although his attitude sometimes seems too patronizing by modern standards. The Gyofū museum in Itoigawa contains some valuable Ryōkan materials. (4)

Sone Chigen (dates unknown): the husband of Ryōkan's sister, Mikako. He was the head priest of the Jōgenji temple in Izumozaki, and known also as the priest Tenge. (34), (83), 161

Sōneiji: a temple in Chiba prefecture, famous during the Tokugawa period. (94)

Sosei (dates unknown): a poet of the *Kokinshū*, and a son of Henjō. His poetry shows aptness of imagery and elegance of diction. (11), (14)

Sugawara no Michizane (845-903): a poet-scholar of the Heian period, who rose to be the Minister of the Right in 899 but lost his position in 901 and died in exile at Dazaifu, Kyūshū. Yet the memory of his wisdom and power was so potent that, after his death, he was feared and worshipped as a divine being (Tenjin). Some people even believed that he escaped death and went to China. He is a leading poet of the *Wakanrōeishū*. (18), 206

Suma: a beach on the Inland Sea, near Kōbe. Together with Akashi, it is particularly famed in Japanese literature for its beauty. 195

Sung: a Chinese dynasty which lasted from 960 to 1126. 92

Su Shih (1036-1101): a poet-essayist of the Sung dynasty; a high official who lived many years of his life in exile. His deeply philosophical poems became popular among the Zen priests of the Kamakura and Muromachi period. (20)

Suzuki Chinzō (1796-1870): a Confucian scholar who opened a school near Yoshida; known also as Bundai. Ryōkan is said to have heard him lecturing on T'ang poetry, and praised him highly. In one of his letters, Bundai says that Ryōkan took the tonsure because he saw the execution of a robber. He also collected Ryōkan's Chinese poems under the title of *Sōdōshū*, and in this edition he says that Ryōkan disliked metrical rules. (21), (35), (51), 153, 268n

Suzuki Ryūzō (d. 1851): an elder brother of Suzuki Chinzō; a physician in a village near Yoshida. Ryōkan thanked him for the gift of some medicine. (51), 152

Tabito: *see* Ōtomo no Tabito.

Tachibana Hikozan (dates unknown): Ryōkan's classmate at Ōmori Shiyō's school, who, according to his brother, discovered that Ryōkan had returned to his native country. (42)

Tachibana Konron (dates unknown): a brother of Tachibana Hikozan; the author of *Hokuetsu Kidan*, in which he describes Ryōkan's life at Gōmoto shortly after his return to his native country. (41)

Tachibana no Moroe (684-757): a famous courtier of the Nara period, who rose to be the Minister of the Left under the Emperor Shōmu and contributed greatly to the construction of the colossal statue of Buddha in Nara. It was believed that Ryōkan's family was descended from him. (30)

Tachibanaya: the name given to the house of Ryōkan's family, deriving from Tachibana no Moroe. (30), (42)

Ta-hsiang: a town in Shantung province where Confucius was criticized by the inhabitants for not being a master of any particular trade. The Japanese name of the town is Takkō. 214

Taibai: *see* T'ai-mêi.

Taichō (683-768): a famous priest of the Nara period, known also as Jinyū; the founder of the Kokujōji temple on Mt. Kugami. He is said to have subdued the thunder god by the power of the *Saddharma Puṇḍarīka Sutra (Hokekyō)*. (44)

Taihaku: see T'ai-po.

T'ai-mêi: a mountain in Chekiang province, where Fa-ch'ang lived; hence his nickname. 111n

T'ai-po: a mountain in Chekiang province, known also as T'ien-t'ung (Tendō), where Dōgen studied Zen under Ju-ching (Nyojō); its Japanese name is Taihaku. 92

Takako: *see* Yamamoto Takako.

Takano: *see* Kōyasan.

Takashima Iemon (dates unknown): the husband of Takako, Ryōkan's sister. (33)

Takemorosumi no Mikoto: the god enshrined at the Otogo shrine, where Ryōkan lived for many years. He is believed to be the youngest son of Ame no Kagoyama no Mikoto, who is enshrined at the Yahiko shrine. (47)

Takizawa Bakin (1767-1848): a romance writer of the Edo period, whose most representative works are *Chinsetsu Yumiharizuki* and *Nansō Satomi Hakkenden*. (4)

Takkō: see Ta-hsiang.

Tamagawa: a post town near Tsuruoka, Yamagata prefecture. 182

Tamashima: a city on the Inland Sea, near Okayama. Here, at the Entsūji temple, Ryōkan studied Zen under Kokusen for more than ten years. (36), (38), 122

Tanabe no Sakimaro (fl. 748): a poet of the *Man'yōshū*, who at one time served as an envoy from Tachibana no Moroe to Ōtomo no Yakamochi. Sakimaro wrote many *chōka* in a relatively plain style. (8), (10)

T'ang: a Chinese dynasty which lasted from 618 to 906. (20), (21) (24), 92, 129

Tanomoan: the name of the cottage situated near Tsubame, where Ugan lived after his retirement. 140n

Tanuma Okitsugu (1719-1788): a *samurai* of the Edo period, who rose to power in 1772 when he was appointed chief of the Council of Elders. He adopted a liberal line, which accelerated the rise of the merchant class and increased social inequality. (43)

T'ao Hung-ching (452-536): a Chinese Taoist, known for his works on occultism, astrology, herbal science, and the beauty of his calligraphy. His Japanese name is Tō Kōkei. 171n

T'ao Yüan-ming (365-427): a poet-essayist of the Chin dynasty, known also as T'ao Ch'ien. Though he served as a minor official, he always yearned for his native country. Eighty days after he was appointed

Magistrate of P'eng-tse, he retired permanently from public life. His poetry, marked by simplicity and idyllic serenity, became popular in Japan. His influence on Ryōkan is perhaps second only to that of Han-shan. (22), (23), (24)

Teichin: *see* Abe Sadayoshi.

Teika: Fujiwara no Teika.

Teishin (1798-1872): the nun who became Ryōkan's faithful disciple in his last years, and the compiler of *Dewdrops on a Lotus Leaf (Hachisu no Tsuyu)*, the earliest anthology of his *waka*. She was a daughter of Okumura Gohei, a minor *samurai* in the service of the feudal lord at Nagaoka. She married Seki Chōun at seventeen, but five years later, when her husband died, she became a nun, and retired to Emmadō in the village of Fukushima. She was twenty-nine and Ryōkan was sixty-nine when they first met in 1827. For about five years, till Ryōkan's death, they maintained a warm relationship and exchanged many poems. (35), (52), (53), (54), 251n, (209)

Tempō: a period name given to the years 1830-1844. (222)

Tendai: *see* T'ien-t'ai.

Tenge: *see* Sone Chigen

Teradomari: a town on the coast of the Japan Sea. The Mitsuzōin temple where Ryōkan stayed for a time was situated here. (33), 221, 387n, 406

T'ien-t'ai: a group of mountains in Chekiang province; an important centre of Buddhism, where traditionally Han-shan and Shih-tê are believed to have lived in seclusion. Its Japanese name is Tendai. (26), 215

Tokō: *see* Yamada Tokō.

Tokugawa: the surname of the *shōguns* of the Edo period. The Tokugawa government, founded by Tokugawa Ieyasu in 1603, lasted till 1867. The period of its rule is called the Tokugawa or Edo period. (20), (30), (42)

Tokushōji: a temple in Yoita, where Daiki was the head priest. 271n

Tomidori Yukinori (dates unknown): Ryōkan's classmate at Ōmori Shiyō's school, a son of the village head of Jizōdō. Ryōkan wrote a poem to mourn his death. 138

Tōren (fl. 1178): a poet of the *Shinkokinshū*. Kamo no Chōmei says of him in *Muyōshō* that, after learning the name of an unusual plant from a teacher, he took special pride in his knowledge. (5)

Tosa: a province in Shikoku, now Kōchi prefecture. Kondō Manjō says that he met Ryōkan in this remote district. (38)

Toyama Shigeemon (d. 1824): the husband of Ryōkan's sister Murako. He was a merchant in Teradomari. (33)

Ts'ao Chih (192-252): a poet of the post-Han period; a son of Ts'ao Ts'ao, the general who paved the way for the founding of the Wei dynasty. Ts'ao Chih was his father's favorite in his youthful years, but was later persecuted by his brother. His poetry expresses tragic emotions. (22)

Ts'ao-hsi: the place in Kwangtung province where Hui-nêng (Enō) taught his disciples, its Japanese name being Sōkei. 51n

Tsu: a province on the east coast of the Inland Sea, now Ōsaka-fu; known also as Settsu. 223, 402

Tzu-lu (b. 543): a disciple of Confucius, famous for his great devotion and courage, his Japanese name being Shiro. 214

Tsunenobu: *see* Minamoto no Tsunenobu.

Tsurayuki: *see* Ki no Tsurayuki.

Tsuruoka: a city in Yamagata prefecture, where Ōmori Shiyō taught in his last years, and Ryōkan visited him. (33)

Tu Fu (712-770): a poet of the T'ang dynasty; one of the greatest Chinese poets. He lived during the turbulent years of the An Lu-shan rebellion, often reduced to near-starvation during his wandering and imprisonment. Legend has it that he died from overeating after he had been rescued from a flood. The happiest years of his life were spent at a thatched cottage in Wan-hua-hsi in the suburbs of Ch'eng-tu, where he was given a minor job by his patron. His poetry reflects his indignation against social injustice, and contrasts sharply with the romanticism of Li Po, in that it is more realistic and objective. Tu Fu is also famous for his technical mastery. (20), (23), (24), (51), 210

Ugan (d. 1808): a priest of the Mannōji temple in Tsubame, who lived after his retirement at the cottage called Tanomoan in the village of Shiniida, not far from Tsubame. He was a close friend of Ryōkan's and shared with him an interest in religion, poetry, and calligraphy. 139, 140

Uji: a city in the vicinity of Kyōto, known during the Heian period as a place of retirement for courtiers, and, in poetry, as a melancholy place because of the pun on its name: *uji/ushi* (melancholy). (16)

Usui: a mountainous pass between Nagano and Gunma prefectures; also the name of the river on its eastern slope, a branch of the Tonegawa river. 195

Vimalakīrti (dates unknown): a rich Indian merchant who became a disciple of Buddha. Although he remained a layman to the end, he exhibited great wisdom and understanding. His Japanese name is Yuima, and the sutra which records his conversation with Mañjuśrī is called in Japanese *Yuimagyō*. 8n, 199

Waka no Ura: a scenic bay in Wakayama prefecture, famous in Japanese literature because of a pun on its name (*waka* meaning "Japanese poetry"). 225

Wang Wei (c.699–c.761): a poet of the T'ang dynasty, famous also for his gifts in painting and music. He was a devout Buddhist and is believed to have been a strict vegetarian. He spent most of his life in Ch'ang-an, serving as an official, although during the An Lu-shan rebellion he was seized and detained in Lo-yang. In his last years, he retired to his country residence at Wang-ch'uan, situated to the southeast of the capital. His poetry is marked by economy of expression, the freshness of its carefully selected details, and a quiet religious atmosphere. His nature poetry is famous for its pictorial quality. (23), (24)

Wan-hua-hsi: a village in the vicinity of Ch'eng-tu where Tu Fu lived in a thatched cottage; its Japanese name is Kankakei. 210

Watanabe: a village near Mt. Kugami, where Abe Sadayoshi was the village head. (49)

Wei: a Chinese dynasty which lasted from 220 to 265. 129

Wei-yen (751–834): a priest of the T'ang dynasty, who taught at Yao shan (Yakuzan) in Hunan province, whence his nickname Yakuzan or Yakkyō. One night when he saw the full moon rise between the clouds, he is said to have laughed so loudly that his laughter was heard ninety miles away. His Japanese name is Igen. 51

Yahiko: a mountain in the Ryōkan country, situated to the north of Mt. Kugami. Ame no Kagoyama no Mikoto is enshrined at the Yahiko shrine at the foot of the mountain. (47), 164, 232

Yakamochi: *see* Ōtomo no Yakamochi.

Yakkyō: *see* Wei-yen.

Yamabe no Akahito (d. c.736): a poet of the *Man'yōshū*, probably a courtier of low rank in the service of the Emperor Shōmu. His poetry is marked by a genuine purity of description. He was praised by Ki no Tsurayuki as a poet ranking with Kakinomoto no Hitomaro. (7), (8), (10), (15)

Yamada Tokō (d. 1844): a *sake* brewer in Yoita; a *haikai* poet. Ryōkan's letter to him written shortly after the earthquake of 1828 is famous. (50), 290n

Yamamoto (Ryōkan's family)

  Yamamoto Jirōzaemon Yasuo (1738–1795): Ryōkan's father. Born in Yoita, he married into the Yamamoto family in 1754. He succeeded his father-in-law as the headman of Izumozaki but proved to be a poor administrator. In 1786, he retired and in 1792, went to live in Kyōto, where, in 1795, he jumped into the Katsura river, committing suicide. He was a distant disciple of Bashō through Shikō and Hokumei, and a friend of Kyōtai. His pen name was Inan. (31), (32), (43)

Yamamoto Hideko (1735-1783): Ryōkan's mother. Born on the island of Sado, she was adopted into the Yamamoto family in 1751, three years before her marriage with Inan. She died in 1783, while Ryōkan was still at the Entsūji temple in Tamashima. (32)

Ryōkan (1758-1831): His boyhood name was Eizō and after his coming of age he was called Fumitaka. He studied at Ōmori Shiyō's school and, following his father, became a local official. Soon, however, he took the tonsure, and entered the Kōshōji temple. In 1779, he went to the Entsūji temple and studied Zen under Kokusen. In 1790, he obtained permission to establish himself as a priest, and left the temple. After spending five years or so as a wandering priest, he returned to his home country. He entered Gogōan in 1804, moving to the Otogo shrine in 1816. He began to live in a cottage attached to Kimura Motoemon's house in the town of Shimazaki in 1826, and died there in 1831. Ryōkan left some fourteen hundred *waka*, four hundred *kanshi*, and a small number of *hokku*.

Yamamoto Murako (1760-1824): Ryōkan's sister, who married Toyama Shigeemon, a merchant in Teradomari. (33)

Yamamoto Shinzaemon Yasunori (1762-1834): Ryōkan's brother. Following his father, he became the headman of Izumozaki in 1786 but through his misgovernment caused the downfall of his family. He was expelled from Izumozaki on charges of misappropriation in 1810. He wrote *waka* under the pen name of Yūshi. Throughout his life, Ryōkan kept the closest contact with this brother. (33), (34), (40), (42), (43), (44), (54), 136, 254n, 270n, 289, 374n

Yamamoto Takako (1769-1812): Ryōkan's sister, who married Takashima Iemon and lived in Izumozaki. (33)

Yamamoto Enchō (1770-1800): Ryōkan's brother, known also as Yūcho. He became the head priest of the Enmeiji temple in Izumozaki. (33)

Yamamoto Kaoru (d. 1798): Ryōkan's brother, who established his fame as a scholar in Kyōto; known also as Tansai. He is said to have lectured on the *Kokinshū* to the Emperor Kōkaku. He also wrote some *kanshi*. (34)

Yamamoto Mikako (1777-1852): Ryōkan's sister, who married Sone

Chigen, the head priest of the Jōgenji temple in Izumozaki, and became a nun under the name of Myōgen. She was a friend of Teishin, and left some *waka*. (34)

Yamamoto Hokuzan (1752-1812): a scholar of the Edo period, who attacked those who imitated T'ang poetry. He was also opposed to the reactionary policy of Matsudaira Sadanobu. (21)

Yamanoue no Okura (c.660-733): a poet of the *Man'yōshū* whose criticism of Buddhist priests living in isolation was to provoke Ryōkan to write a reply. Okura went to China in 701 as one of the followers of the Japanese envoy. He was appointed Governor of Chikuzen province in 726, and became a close friend of Ōtomo no Tabito who was in Kyūshū as Governor of Dazaifu. Okura's poetry is characterized by its strong Chinese flavor, its stark realism, and the roughness of its style. (8), (9), (10), 413

Yamasaki Rakusai (1782-1851): a physician in the village of Wanō near Iwamuro. He was known as an excellent player of the Chinese harp, and named his house Kyūkindō (Harp-resounding House). 282n

Yamato: originally the name of the district around Nara, but soon it came to mean the whole of Japan. 254

Yen-ling (dates unknown): a famous prince of the Ch'un-ch'iu period whose musical knowledge was so great that he was able to distinguish every song in *Shih Ching* on hearing. His Japanese name is Enryō. He was also known as Chi-cha (Kisatau). 196

Yoita: a town on the west bank of the Shinano river, where Ryōkan's father, Inan, was born. Ryōkan's friends, Yamada Tokō and Miwa Gonpei, also lived here. On one occasion Teishin met Ryōkan in this town. (30), (50), (51), 144, (218)

Yonezawa: a city in Yamagata prefecture. Ryōkan stopped here on his way to Tsuruoka where he visited his teacher, Ōmori Shiyō. 181

Yoshida: a town on the east bank of the Saikawa, one of the estuaries of the Shinano river, where Ryōkan's friends Suzuki Ryūzō and Chinzō lived. (51)

Yoshino Hideo (1902-1967): a poet and editor of *Ryōkan Kashū* (Nihon Koten Zensho, Asahi Shinbunsha, 1952) and *Ryōkan Shū* (Koten Nihon Bungaku Zenshū, 21, Chikuma Shobō, 1966). (10), (15), 220n

Yoshiyuki: *see* Yamamoto Shinzaemon Yasunori.

Yūgure no Oka: a hill situated to the southeast of Mt. Kugami. 383n

Yuhara no Ōkimi (fl. 733): a poet of the *Man'yōshū* and son of Prince Shiki. His poetry is marked by quiet description of nature. (10)

Yuima: *see* Vimalakīrti.

Yukinori: *see* Tomidori Yukinori.

Yūshi: *see* Yamamoto Shinzaemon Yasunori.

Yuri (dates unknown): the wife of Sakutarō, a carpenter in Izumozaki. Her devotion to her mother-in-law during the absence of her husband won high praise. The monument built in her honor with an inscription by Hayashi Hōkoku can still be seen in Izumozaki. 209n

Zenkōji: a famous temple in the city of Nagano, which Ryōkan visited twice; the first time with his teacher, Kokusen, and the second time by himself. 180

SELECTED BIBLIOGRAPHY

Early Texts

Teishin, *Hachisu no Tsuyu (Dewdrops on a Lotus Leaf)*, a collection of Ryōkan's Japanese poems, completed in 1835
Hayashi Mikao, *Ryōkan Zenji Kashu (The Priest Ryōkan's Japanese poems),* completed in c. 1857
Zōun, *Ryōkan Dōjin Ikō (The Priest Ryōkan's Posthumous Works)* a collection of Ryōkan's Chinese poems, Shōkodō, Edo, 1867
Kobayashi Jirō, *Sō Ryōkan Shishū (The Priest Ryōkan's Chinese Poems),* Seikadō, Tōkyō, 1883
Kobayashi Jirō, *Sō Ryōkan Kashū (The Priest Ryōkan's Japanese Poems),* Seikadō, Tōkyō, 1892

Early Biographies and Studies

Tachibana Konron, *Hokuetsu Kidan (Strange Stories of North Etsu Province),* Eijudō, Edo, 1811
Ōzeki Bunchū, *Ryōkan Zenji Den (A Life of the Priest Ryōkan)* completed in c.1818
Iizuka Hisatoshi, *Tachibana Monogatari (The Tale of the House of Orange),* completed in c.1843
Kera Yoshishige, *Ryōkan Zenji Kiwa (Strange Episodes of the Priest Ryōkan),* completed in c.1845
Kondō Manjō, *Nezame no Tomo (A Friend in Sleepless Hours),* written in 1845
Gamō Shigeaki, *Kinsei Ijin Den (Lives of Recent Great Men),* Aoyama Kiyokichi, Tōkyō, 1881
Oka Kamon, *Hokuetsu Yūjō (North Etsu Province Visited),* written in 1888

Later Texts

Sōma Gyofū, *Ryōkan Oshō Shikashū (The Priest Ryōkan's Poems, Both Chinese and Japanese)* Shunyōdō, Tōkyō, 1918
Ōtsuka Kasoku, *Ryōkan Zenshū (The Complete Works of Ryōkan),* Iwanami Shobō, Tōkyō, 1924
Yoshino Hideo, *Ryōkan Kashū (Ryōkan's Japanese Poems),* Nihon Koten Zensho, Asahi Shinbunsha, Tōkyō, 1952

Tōgō Toyoharu, *Zenshaku Ryōkan Shishū (Ryōkan's Chinese Poems, Fully Interpreted)*, Sōgensha, Tōkyō, 1962
Tōgō Toyoharu, *Ryōkan Kashū (Ryōkan's Japanese Poems)*, Sōgensha, Tōkyō, 1963
Yoshino Hideo, *Ryōkan Shū (Ryōkan's Japanese Poems)*, Koten Nihon Bungaku Zenshū, 21, Chikuma Shobō, Tōkyō, 1966
Tanigawa Toshiaki, *Ryōkan Shokan Shū (Ryōkan's Letters)*, Nojima Shuppan, Sanjō, 1973
Iriya Yoshitaka, *Ryōkan (Ryōkan's Chinese Poems)*, Nihon no Zen Goroku, 20, Kōdansha, Tōkyō, 1978

Later Biographies and Studies

Nishigōri Kyūgo, *Samon Ryōkan Zenden (A Complete Life of the Priest Ryōkan)*, Meguro Shoin, Tōkyō, 1914
Sōma Gyofū, *Taigu Ryōkan (Ryōkan Foolish and Great)*, Shunyōdō, Tōkyō, 1918
———, *Ryōkan to Issa to Bashō (Ryōkan, Issa, and Bashō)*, Shunjūsha, Tōkyō, 1925
———, *Ryōkan Hyakkō (One Hundred Studies on Ryōkan)*, Kōseikaku, Tōkyō, 1935
———, *Ryōkan to. Teishin (Ryōkan and Teishin)*, Rokugeisha, Tōkyō, 1938
Jacob Fischer, *Dew-drops on a Lotus Leaf*, Kenkyūsha, Tōkyō, 1954
Yoshino Hideo, *Ryōkan no Hito to Uta (Ryōkan and His Japanese Poems)*, Yayoi Shobō, Tōkyō, 1957
Tōgō Toyoharu, *Ryōkan*, Sōgensha, Tōkyō, 1957
Miya Eiji, *Ryōkan*, Sansaisha, Tōkyō, 1969
Karaki Junzō, *Ryōkan*, Chikuma Shobō, Tōkyō, 1971
Takagi Kazuo, *Samon Ryōkan (The Priest Ryōkan)*, Tanka Shinbunsha, Tōkyō, 1973
Imoto Nōichi, *Ryōkan*, Kōdansha, Tōkyō, 1978
Katō Kiichi, *Ryōkan to Teishin (Ryōkan and Teishin)*, Kōkodō, Niigata, 1979

10. Gogōan, the cottage where Ryōkan lived from 1804 to 1816 (reconstructed in 1914).

PRINCETON LIBRARY OF ASIAN TRANSLATIONS

A HISTORY OF CHINESE POLITICAL THOUGHT, *by Kung-chuan Hsiao, translated by* F. W. Mote

POETS OF THE TAMIL ANTHOLOGIES, *translated by George L. Hart III*

TOLD ROUND A BRUSHWOOD FIRE: The Autobiography of Arai Hakuseki, *translated by Joyce I. Ackroyd*

ŌKAGAMI, *translated by Helen McCullough*

HSÜEN YÜEH AND THE MIND OF LATE HAN CHINA: A Translation of the Shen-Chien, *by Ch'i-yun Ch'en*

Library of Congress Cataloging in Publication Data

Ryōkan, 1758-1831.
The Zen poems of Ryōkan.

Bibliography: p.
I. Yuasa, Nobuyuki, 1932- II. Title.
PL797.6.A294 1981 895.6'13 80-8585
ISBN 0-691-06466-0 AACR2

GPSR Authorized Representative: Easy Access System Europe - Mustamäe tee 50, 10621 Tallinn, Estonia, gpsr.requests@easproject.com